LEADERSHIP AND THE ART OF CONVERSATION

D0037519

LEADERSHIP AND THE ART OF CONVERSATION

CONVERSATION AS A MANAGEMENT TOOL

Kim H. Krisco

PRIMA PUBLISHING

Library of Congress Cataloging-in-Publication Data

Krisco, Kim H.
    Leadership and the art of conversation: conversation as a management tool / Kim H. Krisco.
       p.   cm.
    Includes index.
    ISBN 0-7615-1030-3
    1. Leadership. 2. Conversation. 3. Interpersonal communication. I. Title.
HM141.K73 1997   97-15326
303.3'4—DC21

99 00 01 HH 10 9 8 7 6 5

Printed in the United States of America

How to Order
Single copies may be ordered from Prima Publishing, P.O. Box 1260BK, Rocklin, CA 95677; telephone (916) 632-4400. Quan-tity discounts are also available. On your letterhead, include information concerning the intended use of the books and the number of books you wish to purchase.

Visit us online at www.primapublishing.com

The important thing is this. . . .
To be able at any moment to sacrifice what we are
for what we could become.

—Charles DuBois

CONTENTS

ACKNOWLEDGMENTS

My ideas are limited by my experience, nationality, culture, gender, and age. I want to thank my growing international family of friends, clients, and colleagues for teaching and helping me to see and move beyond my personal limitations.

I particularly want to thank my daughter Jennifer for her constant love and great ideas, and for helping me discover and understand the most important leadership quality—selflessness. By being selfless, the leader enhances self.

I also wish to thank Pamela Slader Krisco for helping me come to grips with what is really important in my life—better late then never. And to Sara Ferguson who sees the "Possibility" in me and tugs at it each day.

Finally, I want to thank my other coaches, Bill and Marilyn Veltrop, Mike Barker, Maureen Garrison, Miguel Moreno, Cheryl Laird, James Dowling, Glenn Hunter, Mark Narvaez, and my Tai Chi master Mr. Ho, for making a denim purse out of a sow's ear (a *silk* purse someday).

INTRODUCTION: A PROMISE

Conversation takes many forms. One form of conversation is called a *promise*, and it makes things happen. It creates expectations, the first step toward delivering results. This book comes with a promise:

What you will discover in this book will immediately and dramatically improve your effectiveness as a leader. You will find out how to get more of what you want and need, most of the time.

As you pick up any book for the first time, you can't help but wonder, "Is this book really for me?" In this case, I can answer yes with complete confidence, because the technology presented here can boost your leadership skills quickly and dramatically regardless of their current level of development. A *technology* is a process that, when applied, will deliver a predictable result—and that's what this book does. It gives you a step-by-step process that you can apply to leadership in all aspects of your life.

If you are just beginning to spread your leadership wings, this book is perfect for you. You will learn eight principles that you can apply immediately, and that will immediately make you a more effective leader.

If you are already a successful and accomplished leader, this technology will help you better understand and use the talents you have. When you can do consciously and intentionally what you now do intuitively, your natural leadership ability will become more accessible to you. You will become even more powerful and effective, and you will act more decisively.

I have been using the techniques and processes presented in *Leadership and the Art of Conversation* successfully for the last eight years in my executive coaching practice.

Indeed, the examples and anecdotes you will see through-out the book are taken from my coaching practice—many from transcripts of actual coaching sessions.

Whether you are an established or developing leader, you must cope with situations and circumstances you did not create, and over which you might think you have lit-tle control. However, there is one thing over which you do have total control—the way you speak and listen. By managing the way you speak and listen, you can influence and change even the most difficult circumstances. As George Bernard Shaw said: "People are always blaming their circumstance for what they are. I don't believe in circumstances. The people who get on in this world are the people who get up and look for the circumstances they want, and if they can't find them, make them." This book gives you the principles and skills by which you can find or make the circumstances you want in your life.

While these principles and skills are extremely useful in a business and professional setting, they are equally helpful off the job as well, and both areas are explored in the coming chapters.

You will learn how to:

- Avoid the traps that keep you and others in the mode of producing incremental improvements.

- "Break out of the box" and create possibilities that dramatically shift the direction you and your organi-zation are going.

- Transform your image and change how people per-ceive and treat you.

- Improve your self-esteem and self-image.

- Get everything other people can give to your mutual projects.

- Increase the velocity of positive change in your life and organization.

- Intentionally achieve breakthroughs in all areas of your life.

Using the ideas and principles revealed in this book, people just like you have changed their lives, organizations, families, and communities. They have shaken the world and made it a better place You can do the same . . . and that's a promise.

1

Tapping Your Most Precious Asset

If you observe and compare your daily activities with those of the most noteworthy business leaders, you will find little difference. You hold and attend meetings, plan, send and receive correspondence and phone calls, and so on, just as they do. Despite this similarity, you will often find that the more accomplished leaders achieve greater results more quickly. That's because they're using their most precious asset to its fullest: their ability to use conversation to enlist support and get the people around them involved in creating a fundamentally new future. This hidden asset is the key to unlocking your leadership potential, whether you run a newsstand on Main Street or a corporate office on Wall Street.

It's easy to ignore the value of conversation as an asset. When I ask my clients, "What do you do all day?" they might say, "I direct and supervise others." If I continue to probe, we find out what they *really* do.

> *Me:*   Directing and supervising . . . can you be more precise?
>
> *Client:* My team does research, planning, and analysis.
>
> *Me:*   No, no . . . what do *you* do? *(At this point my clients sometimes hear a veiled indictment—as though I'm saying they do little. But I'm not. I simply want them to discover their own hidden asset.)*
>
> *Me:*   What would you say if your seven-year-old son asked what you do? Remember, he won't understand business jargon.
>
> *Client:* I might say that I manage people.
>
> *Me:*   Okay. How do you do that? Do you take them from place to place, put pens in their hands and help them write memos?
>
> *Client:* I *tell* them. I talk to them about what we should do and how to do it.
>
> *Me:*   You've got it. For you, as for most people, *work is conversation.*

Talk is cheap only if you treat it as cheap. If you use it well, conversation becomes your most precious asset. *Conversation,* as I use the word in this book, includes not only speaking and listening, but writing and reading, verbal and nonverbal behavior, drawing, painting, singing, e-mail, Post-it Notes, and so on. Conversation goes beyond communication—simply getting information from point A to point B—to include the reception and understanding of information.

BASIC TOOLS AND PRINCIPLES

Since leadership manifests in conversation, you can dramatically and immediately improve your ability and effectiveness by changing the kind and frequency of conversations you have. But to do that, you need to be able to discriminate among conversations—that is, to make *distinctions* among them.

Distinction is the first of several useful conversational tools. When you distinguish something you identify it, categorize it, and see it in greater depth and detail. The process of distinguishing creates a new awareness that leads to more precise and measured actions.

The ability to make distinctions is the key to mastery in any area. Being able to distinguish different shades of color and different surfaces will make you a better painter. Being able to distinguish different textures in snow makes you a better skier. Likewise, being able to discern differences in the way you and others speak and listen makes you a more effective leader.

This book is packed with useful and powerful distinctions for conversation. There are kinds of conversations such as *discussions, dialogues,* and *feedback sessions*—words often used in casual speech to mean pretty much the same thing, but here given shades of meaning that let you use them in different ways. Other distinctions include actions performed during a conversation, called *speech acts.* This is a useful group term for *promises, declarations, requests, opinions, assessments,* and so on—words that describe actions that you perform simply by speaking, which is the essence of conversation.

There are eight basic principles of conversation. You'll meet them in detail in the course of this book, and some of the distinctions they include won't mean much yet. However, here they all are in brief so you can see where we're going:

- Be aware of the power of conversation and pay close attention to how you speak and listen.

- Don't dwell on past conversations; use them to establish a connection and then move on.

- Be aware of, manage, and change the broad invisible unspoken conversations that determine the way people see and interpret the world.
- Shift the conversation first from the past to the future and then to the present.
- Manage your listening and that of others by couching and by substituting affirmative for reactive listening.
- Distinguish between those things that exist in substance and those that exist in language, and act appropriately.
- Consciously and intentionally manage and shape your own image as someone people listen to attentively.
- Go for a breakthrough.

MAKING DISTINCTIONS: THE KEY TO MASTERING CONVERSATION

As with any change, changing your conversation begins with awareness. That's why the first of the eight principles in mastering the art of conversation is *Be aware of the power of conversation, and pay attention to how you speak and listen.*

Once you become aware of them, you will see that there are different kinds of conversation—more kinds than you ever realized—and that will allow you to make use of each of them. You'll begin to pick out different approaches you and others take when speaking, notice different emotional levels, discern conversational patterns and pitfalls, and determine whether or not a particular conversation will lead to action. This process of distinguishing differences is the key to mastering conversation, allowing you to perceive things differently and consequently change the way you act and react.

Take selling, for example. Why are some members of a sales team more effective than others? Most of them have the same skill set. Indeed, they usually have the same sales training. They have similar motivation. They share the same information about products, services, and customers. However, there is one difference. The ones at the top see distinctions the others do not. If you talk with these leaders, as I recently did with one of my clients, you will understand and appreciate the power of conversational distinctions:

Me: How do you handle customers who have complaints?

Joe: Most customers have complaints, but not all complaints are equal.

Me: What do you mean?

Joe: There's different kinds of complaining. One kind I call "recreational complaining"—griping for the fun of it. It's a game.

Me: What's another kind?

Joe: There's what I call "complaining for action," where customers are wanting me to correct a problem. They ask by complaining.

Me: How do these distinctions help you?

Joe: I respond differently. With recreational complaining, I join in; with the other, I listen closely and take immediate action.

Joe had more distinctions for complaining, but this is enough for a sample. You can see that having just these two makes him more effective. Indeed, his distinctions for complaining have come in handy in my coaching practice. Which brings up an interesting point, namely that you can "borrow" distinctions from someone else, or (as my client did) make them up. Either way, the more distinctions you find or create in any area, the more masterful you become. And since the key to leadership lies in conversation, having more distinctions for conversation will make you a more effective leader.

Leadership and the Art of Conversation is built upon a simple premise:

If mastery is a product of the distinctions you have, and leadership in action is conversation . . . then leadership mastery is accomplished by finding and developing useful and powerful distinctions for conversation.

Selecting the Right Kind of Conversation

Conversation is your job. And, like any job, the right tool makes it easier. Here are some of the distinctions for conversation types you'll meet in this book:

- Background
- Dialogue
- Discussion
- Coaching
- Complaining
- Completing the Past
- Enrollment
- Feedback
- Past, Present, Future
- Possibility

As I noted earlier, some of these words may well seem to mean the same thing at the moment—but they all really are different. That is, they all describe kinds of conversation that are effective in certain situations, and can be disastrous when used in the wrong place.

Take *discussions*, for example. The word *discussion* is derived from the Latin *discutere*—which means to break apart. In a discussion you and others dissect an idea, situation, or plan to find the good and bad elements. If you want to solve a problem, or find out what went wrong, a discussion is the right tool. However, if you use a discussion when doing a performance appraisal, then what should be a developmental process turns into a critique, a demoralizing experience for both parties. Dialogue—a process of sharing experiences, ideas, and awareness discussed in detail in Chapter 8—would be a better conversational tool for appraisals. The right tool for the right job. Dialogue is a learning tool.

Each day you swim in a sea of conversation. When you regard that sea as an undifferentiated mass, you can still make your way through it—you can, so to speak, dog-paddle through each day, keeping your head out of the water and moving slowly but surely toward your objectives. However, by distinguishing and mastering conversation, you will learn some new conversational swimming strokes that will enable you to cut through your daily work with greater speed and get more of what you want out of your many encounters. One of the most powerful conversational distinctions is related to time.

Controlling Your Place in Time

You experience time travel every time you speak. Take something as simple as the conversation around your coffee pot at the start of the day. If you and your colleagues complain about the morning traffic, you are intellectually and emotionally living in the past. If you talk about possible topics for the upcoming staff meeting, on the other hand, you put yourselves in the future—you begin to create the future. Depending on how you wish to spend your time and what you want to accomplish, it would appear that having a conversation about future possibilities might be more useful and productive than lamenting about traffic jams. But this is only the start.

Being able to discern whether conversations are about the past, the present, or the future not only keeps you from wasting time but, as you will see, it enables you to consciously change or shift the conversation into more useful modes. Instead of talking about what happened, you can make something happen. Instead of talking about what's holding you back, you can propel your enterprise forward. Instead of managing breakdowns, you can achieve breakthroughs. Mastering conversation enables you to meet the primary expectation people have for you as a leader. You'll be able to make new and different things happen faster.

The really nice thing about conversational distinctions is that you can apply them right away, begin making a difference and getting results immediately. For example, you can put this new time distinction for conversation to work at your very next meeting. Other terms may make it easier to do this:

- Let's call the past the realm of *history*.
- The present is the realm of *action*.
- And the future is the realm of *possibility*.

FUTURE	PRESENT	PAST
Realm of POSSIBILITY	Realm of ACTION	Realm of HISTORY

Figure 1-1   This time model provides a useful way to think about and label conversations.

Any time you and others talk about something that has already happened, you are in the past, the realm of history. This isn't a matter of the tense of the verbs you use. For example, the statement "I think the major difficulty we have is the way we're organized," is in the past because it describes how things *have been* organized.

Any time someone makes a statement that generates action, you are in the realm of the present even though the action hasn't happened quite yet. For example, "I'll get you those names and numbers as soon as I get back to my office" is in the present because it influences what is happening or about to happen right now. Such a statement creates action and activity.

Finally, whenever a statement introduces or declares a new possibility—something that does not yet exist—the conversation is in the realm of the future. For example, "What if we construct the display on site, rather than building it in the factory?"

You can use Figure 1-1 as the basis for a conversation-tracking worksheet—just take a piece of paper and draw squares on it labeled like the ones in the figure. To use the worksheet, listen to a conversation in progress and make a hash mark in the appropriate square for each statement that belongs in the past, present, or future realm. The distribution of marks among the circles will tell you where the group's energy went.

If you apply the time-realm worksheet to your next meeting, where do you think most of the marks will show up—in the past, present, or future realm? If the meeting is typical, the majority of statements will be in the past. On average, about 80 percent of the statements in a typical conversation are in the realm of history—talking about what happened, what worked, what didn't, and why. About 15 percent of the statements will be in the present, or the realm of action. That leaves only 5 percent in the realm of possibility—where you create the future. This proportion is not necessarily bad. However, the past is not the place to be if you want to make things happen. It's not the place you want to be as a leader, because leaders focus on the future.

MANAGING CONVERSATIONS

Despite the fact that most conversations are in the past, you are far from helpless. You can manage or shift conversations. The notion of managing conversations may seem strange, until you recall that work *is* conversation. You don't manage people, you have conversations that get them to do things. You don't manage a department or function, you hold ongoing conversations that provide direction. What you really manage, day in and day out, is conversation. In general, you will want to manage conversations so that you shift them out of the past and into the present and future. Figure 1-2 outlines the process.

Conversations in the domain of description, or the past, have limited usefulness. You can't change the past. Past-realm conversations, which will be discussed in greater detail in the next chapter, only provide a foundation for action and possibility. If a conversation remains in the

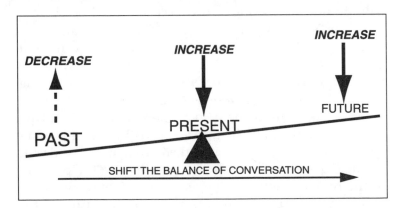

Figure 1-2   Managing conversations means shifting them from the past into the present or the future realm(s).

past, nothing will happen or change. The second principle in mastering the art of conversation is: *Don't dwell on
past-realm conversations; use them to establish a connection and
then move on.*

To shift a conversation out of the past, you simply make
action or possibility statements. By making requests or
declaring a new possibility, you shift the conversation. It
takes time, but with care and persistence you can change
the course of any conversation and get others moving with
you toward a new goal or objective. You may not have
much political clout, but when it comes to conversation,
you are as powerful as anyone.

To give you some idea of how the principles and techniques in this book will enable you to manage conversation, let's take a before-and-after look at a typical business
conversation.

In this scenario the leader is heading up a task team
whose job it is to find the best way to communicate a
major strategic shift and pending reorganization. The
team has only been meeting for a couple of days and
there's little to show. A team member drops by the leader's
office for a casual conversation and is joined by another
team member a bit later. This is how that conversation
might unfold.

Before this book. . . .

Person A: Got a minute?

Leader: Sure . . . what's on your mind?

Person A: We've been through a lot together over the
years, but this assignment takes the cake.

Leader: What do you mean?

Person A: This new strategy is going to wreck this company.

Leader: I don't know if I agree.

Person A: Are you kidding? People aren't dumb. No
matter how we package it, anyone can see

that a lot of people will be out of a job—
maybe you and me.

Leader: It's scary, but we have to find a way to get
buy-in. That's what our team is all about.

Person A: Right . . . the team. Did you pick this team?

Leader: To some extent. We needed a representative
from each unit, but I didn't have contacts
everywhere so—

Person A: You may have reasons for your picks, but
what's with Bob? He's said two words in two
days. He's obviously overwhelmed and out
of his league.

Leader: He's relatively new. I think he's just getting
the lay of the land.

Person A: Or scared to death. Last hired first fired.

Leader: Maybe I'll have a talk with him.

Person A: When you do, you'll find out that his reaction is typical. When people get the message,
there will be shock—quickly followed by
panic.

Leader: I hope you're wrong.

Person A: You know I'm not. We'll dink around for the
next couple of weeks and develop a so-called
plan—employee meetings, special edition
newsletters, etcetera, etcetera. Big deal.
There are only so many ways to get the word
out, and no matter how we package it, it
means trouble.

Person B pokes her head in.

Person B: Am I interrupting?

Person A: No. We could use your opinion. Tell the
truth, what's the bottom line on this new
strategy and reorganization?

Person B: It will make us more competitive and—

Person A: No, no, no. Cut through the B.S. and what do you have?

Person B: Big changes?

Person A: Bottom line it means fewer jobs.

Person B: That's the word on the street.

Person A: Right. And no matter how we candy-coat it, it's bad news.

Leader: I think we have to present the positive aspects of this strategy, too.

Person A: Short and sweet. Just lay it out clear and simple. If we beat around the bush, people will resent it. Frankly I don't know why we even need a team to do this.

After this book . . .

Person A: Got a minute?

Leader: Sure . . . what's on your mind?

Person A: We've been through a lot together over the years, but this assignment takes the cake.

Leader: We *have* weathered some tough times. That's why I wanted you on this team. It's a tough assignment.

Person A: Tough is right. This new strategy is going to wreck this company.

Leader: What makes you say that?

Person A: Reorganization is code for fewer jobs.

Leader: I wouldn't be involved with this project if I thought that. You know I have a low tolerance for B.S. I've been with this firm for over twenty years, and I intend to hang in for the foreseeable future. This strategy can help us do that.

Person A: I'd like to be here twenty years from now too, but I don't think cutting jobs is the way to do it.

Leader: Where are these job cuts you're talking about?

Person A: It's not spelled out, but everyone knows we have to cut costs dramatically.

Leader: And that will make our team's job easier, if people understand why we're changing. And there's more ways to cut costs than just cutting jobs. Those points need to be incorporated into our team's overall communication plan.

Person A: Right . . . the team. Did you pick this team yourself?

Leader: Why?

Person A: You may have reasons for your picks, but what's up with Bob? I don't think he's said two words in two days. He's obviously overwhelmed by this whole process—out of his league.

Leader: Or maybe he's just quiet. If he's overwhelmed, he could use a kind word.

Person A: I got a word for him.

Leader: If that's true then my request may be difficult for you to consider. Would you check in with him at the next meeting . . . make him feel welcome?

Person A: I guess I could do that.

Leader: Will you?

Person A: Sure.

Leader: Thanks. I'm counting on your leadership and experience. I know you can see the positive aspects of this strategy.

Person A: Like what?

Leader: That would be a good question to kick off our next meeting with. Would you lead a discussion of the pros and cons of the strategy?

Person A: I don't know if I'm the right person—

Leader: You're just the right person. I'll set it up and you take over. Will you do that?

Person A: Okay.

Leader: Thanks.

Person B pokes her head in.

Person B: Am I interrupting?

Person A: Just talking about the next meeting.

Leader: We're thinking of beginning by identifying the pluses and minuses of the new strategy.

Person B: The word is that it means job cuts.

Leader: Do *you* believe that's what this is about?

Person B: It doesn't matter what I believe. It's what our people believe that counts.

Leader: What *all* our people believe matters— including you.

Person B: I don't know. I want to believe it's not about job cuts, but I suspect there may be some.

Leader: Possibly, and maybe we need to say that up front.

Person A: Now that would be a first. If we could be frank and honest with people I think we'd have their attention.

Person B: That should be our approach, and it ties in with the pluses and minuses you talked about earlier. Address the minuses head on.

Leader: I think we're on to something. Can you two get the ball rolling at the next meeting by sharing these thoughts? I believe we can break through any skepticism out there and get the support we need for this strategy. Do you agree?

Person A: It would be a breakthrough.

> *Leader:*   Wanna go for it?
>
> *Person A:*   Okay.
>
> *Person B:*   Yeah, let's do it.

Nobody tried to manage the "before" conversation. And like most unmanaged conversations, it stayed in the past and yielded no significant action and no new possibilities for change.

In the "after" conversation, while it dealt with the same people and issues, the leader intentionally shifted the talk from the past to the future. Instead of describing the way things are, the conversation focused on way things *could be.* Also, the leader shaped the way the others viewed him so as to give himself more credibility. Most important, he declared a new future and, through the continual use of requests, put people in action to help implement that view of the future.

This book will make you more aware of your conversations, giving you the power to create a better tomorrow and make things happen today. Most people are totally unaware that, as they speak, they are opening and closing the door to possibility and action. You now have an edge over others. You have a distinction for conversation that enables you to shift conversations through time at will. This alone will often enable you to get what you want. Of course, as with any learning process leading to mastery, the more distinctions you have, and the richer those distinctions are, the more powerful and effective you become.

By distinguishing and intentionally using speech acts, you will be able to keep yourself, your team, and your business growing and prospering. Without these distinctions and conversational tools, the odds are you will be spending too much time in the past—in a survival mode. The next chapter discusses the traps that lie in past conversations and how to avoid them.

2

AVOIDING THE PITFALLS OF THE PAST

We tend to be a product of our past. Much of what we are today, and will be tomorrow, is shaped by what has already transpired in our lives and in the world around us. The future tends to be a continuation of the past, but it doesn't have to be that way. The knowledge and awareness you will gain from this chapter will enable you to break with the humdrum past and create an exciting new future for yourself and your business.

Understanding how the future is created is the most fundamental of leadership skills. Take away everything else, and the essence of leadership is creating and sustaining a viable future.

Envisioning and communicating a new future is a task most people in leadership positions intuitively pursue and accomplish. However, leaders are often puzzled when their vision does not manifest. What many leaders fail to realize is that declaring a new future is only *half* the job. Getting people to let go of the past is the other half.

A vision or new possibility, by itself, does not ensure a new future. The momentum within any organization, and the way most people approach change, tends to stifle efforts to create a dramatically different future. This point became evident during a recent consultation with the owner of a regional training firm—I'll call her Jean.

Jean had decided to grow her 40-person training business into a national enterprise. As she began to plan, she realized that if she wanted to distinguish herself and focus her marketing efforts, she would have to specialize. Looking at the fastest-growing business segment, Jean decided to specialize in computer and software training. She assembled her top managers to create a new mission and vision statement and to develop a business plan.

By most standards, the initial meeting to create a new vision and plan was successful. During one day-long meeting, the group agreed on a vision statement and set up teams, including all employees, to flesh out the business and operating plans. At first, everyone seemed excited and energized by the opportunities and challenges. However, the process began to bog down. Jean held two additional meetings to accelerate the planning process.

When I was invited in, the task teams had been meeting for about three months with little to show. Preliminary reports, recommendations, and plans were disappointing. Jean was stumped. People still seemed committed to the vision, but they were a long way from going into action. Jean asked me, "What's going on, and how can I stop it?"

I explained that most people initially cope with change by consciously or unconsciously slowing it down or incrementalizing it. As exciting as the vision is, it bodes dramatic change—a totally new possibility. As a result, her employees' normal and natural reaction is to step on the brakes. I noted that even unsatisfactory current circumstances seem preferable to an exciting but uncertain future. In short, Jean's employees were clinging to the past. However, breaking from the past is relatively easy if you have the awareness, distinctions, and the right conversational tools. Why conversational tools? Because, as you will see, it is the way people talk that keeps them and their organization in the past.

OVERCOMING THE POWER OF THE PAST

After my initial consultation with Jean, I asked if I could sit in on some of the task team meetings. It turned out that the marketing team was meeting that afternoon. Jean introduced me to the team and took the opportunity to plug the vision and encourage her people. As I listened, I heard the familiar drone of people lost in the past.

Jean: We have what it takes to be a national company. Some of the best marketing minds are in this room. I know you'll find the best way to break into this new, lucrative market.

Person A: One look at the letters coming in tells us that our quick turnaround on projects is our real strength. I think it's our primary differentiator.

Person B: But we'll be playing in a different league now. It's price . . . we have to be price competitive. We're not that good at keeping costs down. Our costs this year grew faster than our revenues.

Person C: You're right, and we were over budget on almost a quarter of our projects. We won't be able to compete with the big guys on price. Niche marketing is the way to go.

Person A: Regardless of the niche, we have to provide good service and turnaround. I've been with this company from the start, believe me price isn't an issue. Let's stick with what we do best.

This meeting was typical of most. The majority of speech acts were in the past. An endless string of opinions, assertions, assessments, interpretations, analyses, evaluations, judgments, beliefs, deductions, and appraisals about the vision, the way the company operates, the way to go, strengths and weaknesses, and so on and on.

You might notice that, in addition to being based on the way things "are," all these statements are subjective. In general, the more subjective a speech act or statement is, the less useful it is in making decisions, solving problems, or creating a future.

Opinions are the most subjective of the speech acts. As such, they are almost totally useless. When one of the team members said, "We have to be price competitive," another responded with "We must pursue niche marketing." It doesn't matter who's right or wrong. All one opinion gets you is another opinion.

If you observe *any* business or personal conversation, you will find that it largely consists of opinions. The provocative nature of opinions is such that once one opinion is offered you can count on hearing from everybody else before you move on. This wastes a lot of time. However, poor use of time is only one of the downsides to past-realm conversations.

Opinions, or any other speech act based in the past, does not create new openings for action, or put people in action. That's why no solid plans were forthcoming from the marketing task team.

To be sure, some speech acts associated with the past, the realm of history, do offer limited benefit. Let's look at a some of these backward-looking speech acts.

- An *assessment* is an opinion based upon facts. For example, the facts are that, in unsolicited letters received by Jean's training company, customers seem to appreciate the quick turnaround on projects. That's a useful fact. However, the assessment that follows—that quick turnaround is the company's strength—is an unsubstantiated opinion. However, it was presented as a fact. If the team were to take action based on the belief that quick turnaround was their key to success, and that assessment was wrong, the consequences could be disastrous. As crazy as this sounds, this kind of stuff happens all the time.

- Likewise, an *interpretation* is the combination of a number of facts to create a hypothesis or story about what has happened or is happening. In the discussion quoted earlier, people presented as fact the information that costs were increasing faster than revenues and that the company was over budget on projects. This information may well be true—spiraling costs and budget overruns are an unfortunate reality of business life. However, even if these two statements do reflect facts, it doesn't necessarily point to the need to do niche marketing. *Deductions* are another form of interpretation. They involve stringing together several related or unrelated facts and drawing a conclusion from them. Depending on the number, accuracy, and quality of the facts, interpretations and deductions can be useful when decisions must be made and all the facts are not available.

- An *assertion* is an opinion based upon some evidence, usually personal experience. "I've been with this company from the start. Believe me, price is not an issue," is an example of an assertion. How useful an assertion is depends on the expertise and integrity of the person making it.

- *Evaluations, analyses, judgments, appraisals,* and most of the other past-realm speech acts can be defined in similar ways. Each is some combination of fact and opinion. As such, each brings with it some usefulness as well as some potential for trouble. However, as stated earlier, the more serious problem with conversations stuck in the past domain is not what they do, but what they don't do. Past conversations do not facilitate action or create new possibilities upon which you and others can take action.

Even if the assessments, interpretations, analyses, assertions, and the rest are accurate, the action that will follow from such a conversation will usually produce little progress and marginal results. This is because action based upon what already exists will create something that looks pretty much the way it does today.

CHANGE BY INCHES: MORE, BETTER, DIFFERENT

Creating a future that is a logical extension of the past is not something that happens from time to time. It is our normal way of operating. Take Jean's employee meetings, for example. The initial one-day meeting was typical. Jean shared her thoughts and ideas for the future. Next, a few of the key managers made speeches of support and announced the task teams. Employees broke into smaller groups to give input to the vision statement and started planning. However, when progress didn't meet expectations, Jean held additional meetings. Not surprisingly, the next meeting was different.

When you make change, your first inclination will be to do more of what you are already doing. In this case, more meetings. And, if that doesn't seem sufficient, you will do it better. Better in Jean's case meant bringing in a professional trainer to plan the meeting, present some planning tools, and facilitate discussions. She also threw in a dinner afterward for employees and their families.

When it became apparent that the second meeting hadn't speeded up the planning process, Jean pulled out all the stops. The third meeting was dramatically different from the previous two. She and her management team went on a retreat in Colorado. Sparing you the details of the retreat, the point is that the typical way we change is via a progression from more to better to different. There is nothing wrong with this per se. It creates change, but usually only incremental change. In most circumstances, doing something more, better, or different will only yield improvements of 10 percent or 15 percent. If that is not sufficient, you need to change the conversation and stop taking action based on opinions.

When Jean's initial meeting didn't deliver the desired result, she seems to have decided that the group needed more structure. At any rate, that's what the decision to hire a professional trainer often implies. In reality, the meeting did not need structure as much as someone to manage the conversation—and you don't need a facilitator to do that.

When the second meeting didn't get acceptable results, Jean laid the blame at the feet of her managers and planned a retreat to get them to confront the issues. Again, she acted based on her opinion or assessment—an internal conversation rooted in the past. Each meeting was successful to a degree. That is, there was some progress, though only a little. However, these meetings, all driven by past conversation, were also creating another problem for Jean—a trap called the endless cycle.

BREAKING THE ENDLESS CYCLE

As we have seen, any time you take action based on opinions, assessments, and interpretations, the best you can hope to achieve is incremental change. However, what is worse, in some situations you will unknowingly take actions that perpetuate the situation or problem you're trying to change. This is called an endless cycle.

In Jean's case, her employees interpreted the succession of big meetings—three within three months—as a sign that the planned expansion of the company was in jeopardy. The second meeting made them suspect that expansion plans might be abandoned, and the third enhanced that suspicion. As a consequence, they put less and less time and energy into the planning process as Jean put more and more energy into getting them to plan, fueling a classic endless cycle like the one in Figure 2-1.

The employees' interpretation (from the past) that the new strategy was in trouble drove their action (in the present)—or in this case, their lack of action. Employees worked less on the new strategy, feeling their time was being wasted. This slowdown worried Jean, who held additional meetings—which tended to confirm employee suspicions and cause them to slow down even further. The meetings Jean hoped would solve the problem ended up exacerbating it.

The endless cycle is undoubtedly at work in your business today. Indeed, it's driving many of your biggest problems. Lack of teamwork, poor union-management relations, diversity issues, and poor employee performance are some areas where you will usually find an endless cycle spinning quietly and nastily along. While you un-

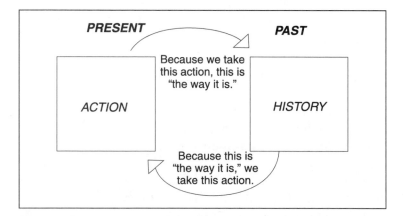

Figure 2-1　The endless cycle, a kind of self-fulfilling prophecy, happens when you take action based on "past conversations."

doubtedly are taking action to resolve these and other problems, you may well also be helping to create them by the way you and others speak and listen.

Let's take the example of an employee or colleague who "is" a poor performer (notice the "is" in quotes). Whenever you use or hear the word *is*, you would be advised to pause and think, because this word is used to transform opinions into facts. "Is" came up a lot in a coaching session I had with a construction foreman trapped in an endless cycle—see the sidebar on the next page headed *He's a Bum.*

The endless cycle is a trap initially created when people mix facts and opinions as they speak and listen. It's difficult to see because opinions are spoken as the truth. Nobody says, "*I would assert that* the union doesn't care about the company." They just say, "The union doesn't care" as though it's a fact. They're not trying to deceive anyone, it's just the way people talk. However, as unintentional and innocent as it may appear, mixing facts and opinions creates many problems for you and everyone else. For Jean, it nearly jeopardized her effort to transform her company.

The fact was that definitive plans were not coming from employee task teams. Her opinion, first that the planning processes needed more structure, and later that the lack of action was the fault of her managers, made her act in ways that slowed the planning process even further. Jean was able to break the endless cycle and get her initiative back on track once she became aware of how she was contributing to the problem.

Me:	Do you believe in taking action based on one person's opinion?
Jean:	Hell no!
Me:	Good. What's holding things back now?
Jean:	My managers. They manage the human resources and the task teams. I'll get them whipped into shape.

> *Me:* What just happened?
> *Jean:* What do you mean?
> *Me:* What did you just say? What was that?
> *Jean:* *(Long pause.)* An opinion. An opinion that sent me off half-cocked.

That was a turning point for Jean, she caught herself in the endless cycle and shifted the conversation going on inside her, as well as the conversation she was having with others. Jean shifted the conversation into the future and present. She created a totally new possibility by trans-

---

He's a Bum

> *Me:* So tell me about this person who gives you heartburn.
>
> *Foreman:* What can I say? He's a bum. *(An opinion spoken as a fact.)*
>
> *Me:* Really? What makes you say that? *(Attempt to separate fact from opinion.)*
>
> *Foreman:* A real pain. He was up for my job. Didn't get it. He wants to make me look bad. *(More assessment and interpretations—description from the past.)*
>
> *Me:* What does he do? *(Try again to get at the facts.)*
>
> *Foreman:* Not much. He's slow . . . takes him twice as long to do anything. And talk about attitude. The guy has all the charm of a snake. *(Got a few facts with interpretations sprinkled in.)*
>
> *Me:* So how do you handle him? *(Want to show his actions are driven from his interpretations.)*
>
> *Foreman:* I stay on his ass every minute. I tell him exactly what to do, how to do it, and when it's to be done. It's the only way.
>
> *Me:* Would you be surprised if I told you that you may be contributing to this situation? *(Trying to shift him into the present.)*

forming the task teams into self-managed operations teams responsible for profit and loss results. This not only put the project back on track, but fundamentally changed the way her company operated.

While Jean made mistakes along the way, we shouldn't be too hard on her. You and I speak and operate out of the past too much of the time ourselves. When we don't manage the way we speak and listen, we waste time and energy. If we're lucky we still make incremental improvements. However, sometimes the actions we take feed the problem we want to solve. If we continue in this mode,

Foreman:	I don't buy it. I inherited this problem child. It's not me. This guy was a bum before I came, and he's still a bum. *(Defensively jumps back into the past.)*
Me:	You didn't *cause* the situation, but you may be contributing to it. *(Gently pull him back into the present.)* Let me ask you . . . if your boss told you what to do, and how to do it . . . if he watched your every move, how would you feel?
Foreman:	I know where you're going with this.
Me:	Humor me. How would you feel? What would you do?
Foreman:	My boss doesn't have to do that. But if he did, I'd quit.
Me:	What if you couldn't quit?
Foreman:	I'd be pretty pissed. I don't know what I'd do. *(He's beginning to see the vicious circle.)*
Me:	Okay, but you'd make trouble, and you'd likely have a bad attitude.
Foreman:	Maybe so. *(Finally have him firmly in the present. As coaching continues, I'll shift him into the future and create a new possibility for him and the problem worker.)*

over time our lack of progress causes poor morale, low productivity, and a host of other leadership nightmares.

Unless you learn to recognize, manage, and shift out of past-realm conversations, you will never be able to deliver on your fundamental responsibility as a leader—creating and sustaining a viable future. However, managing past conversations is more tricky than it might appear.

While managing and shifting past conversations includes reducing the number of opinions, assessments, interpretations, and the like during discussions, there is more to it. Thinking from and speaking from the past is the normal and natural way human beings operate. Having past conversations is automatic and deeply ingrained in each of us. However, managing past conversations is easier with some additional distinctions. With that in mind, let's further distinguish past conversations and explore one of the most insidious ones—*unspoken conversations.*

3

MASTERING THE MOST POWERFUL OF CONVERSATIONS

———

One of the most memorable conversations in my life occurred in 1960. I was fourteen. A friend and I had wandered into what I later found was the last beatnik coffeehouse in Chicago's Old Town. There I met my first *real* beatnik—Felix. He didn't look like the TV stereotype—no sunglasses, no beret, no bongos. But Felix and I talked for hours. One of the most vivid exchanges occurred when I asked Felix what the beat movement was about.

> *Felix:* It's about answering the *big* questions—who am I, where am I going, what's life, what's it all about, Alfie.
>
> *Me:* You get the answers here?
>
> *Felix:* No. You don't. That's the point. But you'll get the answers out there, and they won't be *your* answers. One day you'll wake up and find you're living your father's life.

I didn't realize then, but Felix was talking about one of the most common and insidious conversations around—the unspoken conversation.

Conversations don't always involve face-to-face meetings among people, they can be shared by groups and organizations and proceed largely within the members' minds. These shared conversations dramatically shape every aspect of your life and much of your behavior. Unspoken conversations tell you what's important, what to believe, who's good and who's bad, and so on. They even tell you who you are.

These conversations can be shared by two or three people, or by millions. The purpose of these mostly invisible conversations is to control or influence your behavior. As Felix put it, they "keep your hair trimmed, your beard trimmed, and your mind trimmed." You don't have background conversations, they have you. However, by distinguishing these powerful past-realm conversations, you'll be able to reduce their influence.

Awareness is your primary defense against being used by unspoken conversations. As a leader, you have to guard against their influence, and keep them from influencing those you lead. A leader makes change; unspoken conversations maintain status quo. As a result, being able to deal with them is a quintessential leadership skill.

Discovering What Happens in the Background

Unspoken conversations are so pervasive you don't notice them. We've all heard the expression *not being able to see the forest for the trees*. Unspoken conversations are *not being able to see the trees for the forest*. However, there are times when "background conversations" surface.

Unspoken conversations become obvious if you behave the wrong way—that is, contrary to the assumptions built into the unspoken conversation for what you're doing. For example, a common unspoken conversation in the newspaper or magazine business is that you don't go home until the edition or issue is "put to bed." On deadline day no one asks if they should stay late or work overtime. It's expected. I recall, as a student intern at a local paper, taking off before the edition went to press. I didn't understand the cold shoulder I got the next day until a friend clued me in. However, you don't have to screw up to gain access to unspoken conversations. They bubble up in your business whenever a new person comes on board.

Any newcomer, regardless of skill and experience, needs to know the unwritten rules—what's important in your business, what it takes to be successful, what gets you in the doghouse, all the important stuff. Indoctrinating a new person into your work group and organization is a process of sharing unspoken conversations. What do you tell a new person over a drink at the end of the first day on the job? Those are your unspoken conversations.

I can still recall some of the advice and counsel I got 20 years ago, when I joined a top-50 corporation:

- "You'll get ahead quickly if you put in the hours. The top performers put in sixty hours a week."
- "You might want to get a couple of really top-notch suits. Tailored shirts wouldn't hurt."
- "If you don't achieve a result, be sure you have a damn good excuse. It's possible to excuse your way up the corporate ladder."

While unspoken conversations like those shared during the honeymoon phase of a new job are sometimes spoken, most times they're not. For example, no one told me in my corporate indoctrination that it was important to play a decent game of golf, or to be willing to move every two years. Everyone else was a party to this conversation, which showed up as a wink and a nod, rather than in words. I learned these things the hard way. Sitting at the golf awards program during my first annual conference, the boss leaned over and murmured, "So you decided to sit out the golf game . . . *not* a good idea."

Unspoken conversations, whether in your work or personal life, maintain status quo. In an organization or society, they are seen as providing needed stability and reassurance that the group, organization, or business will survive and continue. Despite, and in part because of, this stabilizing influence, unspoken conversations limit new possibilities and make change difficult. Remember how difficult it is, for instance, to change traditional company policies and practices. However, it's not hopeless.

Managing or Shifting Unspoken Conversations

For the most part, you and I don't start unspoken conversations. They are usually well under way long before we arrive on the scene. Because they're ongoing, we tend to get swept up in them and, as pointed out earlier, used by them. We sometimes find ourselves believing and saying things we've never really thought through. We tend to swallow unspoken conversations whole because we don't see them as conversations. They present themselves to us as the way the world *is*. As with all past conversations, the opinions, assessments, and interpretations implicit in unspoken conversations are spoken as the truth. And because they are, they can be very insidious.

If you are a woman in business you undoubtedly know about the *glass ceiling*—a condition that makes it nearly impossible for a woman to get one of the top jobs. The glass ceiling is an unspoken conversation. A mostly unspoken conversation that says "women can't cut it, they're not as committed, they won't get the respect they need to lead, so there's no point in wasting time putting one in that job." It's called the glass ceiling because it's invisible. As strange as it sounds, the men in the organization are the ones used by this conversation. However, it is the women who have to live with the result—subtle behavior that keeps them from making it into the executive ranks.

If you don't recognize and question unspoken conversations, you become vulnerable to their control. However, now that you have a distinction for them, you are more likely to notice them. Awareness gives you the opportunity to change "the way it is." And you *can* change unspoken conversations.

The third principle you must apply to master leadership conversation is: *Be aware of, manage, and change the broad invisible background conversations that determine the way people see and interpret the world.*

Changing or shifting unspoken conversations is first a matter of recognizing when you are caught up in one. Then begin speaking from the present or future domain of time. You'll get specific speech acts and conversational tools needed to shift the conversation in the chapters that follow. For now it is only necessary that you *distinguish* unspoken conversations. It's worth repeating: A clear distinction is the prelude to awareness, and awareness is the first step in mastering the art of leadership conversation.

Recognizing unspoken conversations and appreciating the power they hold over you and others will transform your worldview and enable you to "break out of the box."

Breaking Out of the Box

You have probably heard the expression "out of the box." James Adams popularized it in his 1974 book *Conceptual Blockbusting.* In general, getting out of the box means operating outside the assumptions, beliefs, values, and ideas that determine how you see and experience the world.

You have a worldview, an explanation for how the world operates. We all do. My worldview assumes such things as: nearly all people are good, learning and loving are what life is about, and the pen *is* mightier than the sword. Your own unique worldview is mostly created in unspoken conversations shared with your parents, teachers, friends, and loved ones, as well as from books, movies, TV, and other outside sources of information and insight. Your personal experiences also shape your worldview, but not as much as you might think.

Unspoken conversations are so powerful that most of the time your experience either confirms the unspoken conversation or gets invalidated. When people encounter an event that contradicts an unspoken conversation, they usually disregard it as a fluke. I ran into a clear example in a coaching session with an executive who was struggling to fill an upper-level position—while in the grip of a "glass ceiling" unspoken conversation:

Me: Who's on your candidates list?

Client: If I decide to stay on the inside, I've got two. One's a woman.

Me: Can she do the job? *(Encouraging him to examine the background conversation about women.)*

Client: I only worked with her once and she did a good job . . . worked well with people, put in the time, delivered what she promised.

Me: Sounds like a winner. You gonna give her the job?

Client: Well, reports are that, overall, she's really an average performer. *(He invalidates his own experience and holds the background conversation as the truth.)*

Me: But you just said—

Client: She was probably pulling out all the stops when she worked with me. I have to wonder if she could sustain that performance. *(Rationalizes— that is, makes up a story to account for the discrepancy between the background conversation and his own experience.)*

I fear my client and his company lost a great vice president. The unspoken conversation limited his thinking and his actions. It put him "in a box." Taken together, all the unspoken conversations we inherit—and those we acquire through experience—become our paradigm, the box we live in. This box is invisible. We don't see our worldview as a story about the way the world operates. To us it's the way the world *is*. There's an ancient Chinese saying that speaks to this point:

There are three great mysteries in life.
Water to a fish.
Air to a bird.
And man to himself.

If a fish could talk, do you think it would say, "Gee it's great to be in the water." No. The fish assumes the world *is* water. It is only because we are standing outside the fish tank that we can see the fish swimming in water. Likewise, it is difficult for you to see the paradigm you swim in— your box.

You bump into the edges of your box whenever you encounter a new belief or idea that disturbs you in some way. Sometimes you will even have a physical or gut level reaction. That's because a clear worldview provides direction for your actions and ultimately provides meaning to your life. Anything that challenges your worldview disturbs you at your very core. For that reason, you may not even hear a conversation that contradicts or challenges your worldview. Or if you do hear it, you will likely reject the information as "wrong." Whenever you or others see things as black or white, right or wrong, you can bet that unspoken conversations have a hold on you. Right-wrong thinking is common,

and it may stem from one of the most ancient background conversations.

ESCAPING THE "RIGHT-WRONG" TRAP

Just as a coffee maker makes coffee and a lawn mower cuts
grass, it would seem that human beings make themselves
right and other people wrong. This right-wrong thinking
is so prevalent and strong because, in a way, our survival
depends on it.

Right-wrong thinking has its roots in a time almost two
million years ago, when our distant ancestors lived in
caves. Back then, existence was about staying alive. It was
literally about survival. Nearly every decision human
beings made then could and would determine whether
they lived or died. If they were wrong about how swift the
river current was, they would be swept away and drowned.
If they were wrong about whether or not to throw a spear
or use a club to hunt, they might starve. If they were wrong
about whether or not a certain plant was edible, they
could be poisoned and get sick or die. Two million years
ago, being right meant surviving.

Today, with a few exceptions—people whose lives really
are on the line moment by moment, like soldiers or police
officers—your physical survival does not depend on
whether or not you are right. But your psychological and
emotional survival does. Who you are—your identity, your
ego, the person you consider yourself to be—is predicated
on a need to be right about nearly everything.

When someone says, "You're wrong," you take it personally, don't you? You can feel the hair stand on the back
of your neck, or maybe a knot forms in the pit of your
stomach. The prospect of being wrong works at your very
core. So much so, that most people would rather be right
than happy. Indeed, some people would rather die than

accept being wrong. That thought occurred to me when I saw one of the most famous gravestones in the world in a cemetery in New Orleans. Under the name and dates it simply said, "I told you I was sick."

With this in mind, is it any wonder that we *must* be right about the way it "is"? Is it any wonder why we cling to un-spoken conversation, and why all past conversations that create our worldview are so difficult to manage and shift? Breaking out of the box begins with a willingness to be wrong. For starters, you must be willing to be wrong about yourself. If I told you could be a millionaire in five years (assuming you aren't one already), what would you think and say? Those are unspoken conversations. Are they the truth? Are they helping you succeed, or holding you back?

If you were to say that your business could double in size in the next two years, what would your colleagues and employees say? Are they helping your enterprise grow—or holding it back? Those are the unspoken conversations you have to manage as a leader.

You can leverage the helpful unspoken conversations by simply giving voice to them, and change the ones under-mining your success. Once you're willing to be wrong, you can begin to use future conversation to create new possi-bilities and go in new directions. You'll learn exactly how do this in the next chapter.

4

CREATING THE FUTURE

It's a good idea to explore and understand the future, because that's where you'll spend the rest of your life. However, if you're like most people, you haven't thought much about what the future really is.

We refer to the future as a place in time, as if time were a road that we travel. But if time were a road, the present would be the end of the road, and that construction mess in the distance would be the future. In other words, the future is always in the making. The future is not a place. The future cannot be encountered or discovered. The future is created—created in conversation.

We've established that the ultimate objective of leadership is creating and maintaining a long-term viable future. Therefore, the ability to create the future is integral to leadership development.

LIVING IN THE FUTURE

As a leader you will be living more of your life in the future, while the people you lead stay mostly in the past or present. Your job is to think ahead, after all, and draw the outlines of the future for your group. That's an exciting effort, and the future is an exciting place to be. In the future, anything is possible—things like walking on the moon, for example.

Back in the sixties, President John F. Kennedy announced that we would put people on the moon and safely return them to earth by the end of the decade. You may not have been born then, but if you were, you may recall that when President Kennedy made that statement there was little evidence that a manned lunar landing was even remotely possible. The Russians had completed several successful space shots. America was behind in the space race. We could barely get a rocket off the launch pad, let alone put someone on the moon. Many scientists at the time said a moon landing was impossible, because we didn't have the fuel and computer technology to make it happen. However, the world watched in awe when, on July 20, 1969, astronaut Neil Armstrong took that "giant step for mankind" and planted an American flag on the moon.

Without discounting the monumental effort put forth by NASA and others, putting a man on the moon can be traced back to that single statement Kennedy made on May 25, 1961. John F. Kennedy *literally* spoke a manned lunar landing into existence. If he, or some other leader, had not made that promise, it would never have happened.

How Future Conversations Work

The moon shot is a spectacular event and the president of the United States is a powerful person, but there are everyday examples of speaking the future into existence all around us.

I'm now working with a book distributor who caters primarily to new-age bookstores. The customer base is growing slowly, but my client Teri wants to tap what she sees as an enormous hidden potential—business customers. As you may know, business books are the biggest segment of the nonfiction book market. However, few businesspeople frequent new-age bookstores.

When I met her, Teri was trying to determine the best way to move her company and her bookstore clients in this new direction. "I've thought about this for a while, and I feel serving mainstream businesspeople is the best way to grow our business. But it's a tough sell. How should I begin?"

"Have you shared this idea with anyone else?" I asked.

"A few," she replied.

"Then you've already begun," I said.

We all intuitively know that the future begins with a conversation—first within our heads, then with others. However, when you plan and hold conversations more consciously and intentionally, you become far more effective. As I worked with Teri, and later with others on her management team, we focused not only on how to more powerfully speak the future, but also about ways to share and expand the conversation to include employees and customers.

Within a matter of weeks, every employee working with Teri was finding ways to attract businesspeople to client stores. That's how a new possibility manifests and the future is created. Everything that you create begins with a conversation that grows and grows. And the action that follows is based on a new possibility, not the past. In the midst of the planning activities, and at the grand opening of a new business section at their biggest customer's store, it might be easy to forget that it all began with a conversation—first in Teri's head, then around the coffee pot and conference table at work.

Without a totally new possibility to drive action, by default, action is driven from the past domain into the more-better-different trap. As indicated earlier, if past conversations drive action, you will tend to make incremental improvements. In Teri's case, until she launched a new possibility, the business plan called for her business to grow by moving into international markets. To be sure, this plan would have yielded additional revenues, but she would still be firmly entrenched in the slower-growing new-age book market.

The Language of the Future

Just as there are specific speech acts such as opinions, assessments, and interpretations associated with the past, there is a speech act associated with the future. It is called a *declaration*. This term sounds very grand, and it can be. President Kennedy's declaration that we would put someone on the moon was a bold statement. However, a declaration can also be quite unassuming. It can take many forms, and include such phrases as:

- "What if—"
- "I think it's possible to—"
- "This team is capable of—"
- "We will become leaders in—"
- "I believe we can—"

When you speak or hear a statement that begins like one of these, a new possibility is being created, and a new future is in the making. As you share a new possibility with others, the conversation can grow. As it does, any action that follows will be driven by the new possibility, and not the past. This is the essence of managing and shifting conversations, and the primary task of a leader.

MANAGING FUTURE CONVERSATIONS

Launching a future conversation is easy; just declare a new possibility. However, maintaining that conversation

is extremely difficult, as any accomplished leader will
tell you.

As you recall, the majority of conversations you hold
and participate in are past conversations; and the "drift" of
conversations is almost always to the past. Let's take Teri's
wholesale book business. I was introduced to her management team as a consultant who would help them explore and, if it seemed viable, initiate a new strategic focus
on business customers. As I expected, Teri's new possibility was greeted with a flurry of conversation from the
past—although it was well camouflaged (as it often is). I
jotted down some of the statements, thinking I would re
fer to them later on. I heard such things as:

- "It would be nice if we could tap the business market,
  but business and metaphysical subject matter are oil
  and water."
- "It makes a lot of sense, but I'm not sure book store
  owners and managers will buy it. A lot of them are corporate dropouts."
- "I'm for it personally, but we've already told our sales
  team and customers that we're going international.
  I'm concerned we'll be sending mixed messages."

You will note that no one openly turned thumbs down on
the idea. Instead they used opinions, assessments, interpretations, and old unspoken conversations to invalidate
the possibility. Since this reception was predicable, I had
prepared Teri. Prior to meeting with her team for the first
time, I had outlined the steps Teri could take to manage
the conversation:

First, using her new distinctions for time realms and
speech acts, Teri was able to see that the conversation was
firmly rooted in the past. This kept her from becoming
defensive and from being sucked into the conversation
herself.

Next, based on her new appreciation for future conversations, she continued to declare her new possibility. Teri

interjected such statements as, "I don't know how, but I think if anyone can figure a way to attract mainstream business and professional people, we can."

In other words, she shifted the conversation from the past to the future by continuing to make declarations. It might be more accurate to say she *began* to shift the conversation. For the conversation will almost inevitably drift back to the past. Indeed, in response to Teri's declaration that their team could find a way to make it work, one member piped up with, "Whether or not we can is not the issue. Two years ago, when we tried to market music, our customers told us they didn't want to sell CDs. Do we really think they want to get into business books?"

In other words, Teri's declaration was invalidated. Usually someone dredges up an incident from the past to make a case against the possibility being offered. But Teri didn't give up. She repeated steps one and two and again, introducing another declaration, with more fervor and details. She said, "Our customers sell books, including business books, to all kinds of people, including business-people. It's a matter of focus and priority. Imagine what would happen if instead of focusing on the new-age readers, who account for about 9 percent of the market, we focus on business readers, who account for almost 32 percent of the market?"

However, even this eloquent challenge was once again greeted with what might be called a *conversation for no possibility*—more opinions, assessments, and interpretations. Teri tried again and again.

It took many efforts, multiple declarations, and more than an hour, but eventually Teri begin to connect with some of the people on her team. They let go of the past and joined in her future conversation, oftentimes building on it. "Yeah, we're not asking our customers to get into a new business, but to expand one high-potential segment of their existing customer base."

As people joined in, the conversation grew larger and stronger. The conversational seeds Teri planted through her repeated declarations grew and sprouted additional possibilities. Her management team begin to take action on the possibility she initially created. For example, before the initial meeting ended, one member of the management team suggested that they go into customers' stores and identify the business-oriented books already on the shelves to point out the potential of this new marketing strategy. However, that was only a start.

It took three months of planning and preparation before one of their biggest stores launched the first pilot project for them. Teri, her employees, and her customers all had a new future. And it all started with a statement, a new possibility, a declaration. That's what it takes to shift or manage a conversation—awareness, the interjection of the appropriate speech act, and perseverance.

LEADERSHIP AND THE DOMAIN OF THE FUTURE

If you do not assert your leadership and use your new distinctions and conversational tools, it is doubtful any fundamental change or growth will happen in your business. Even if colleagues and employees want to break out of the endless cycle and take action, without your intervention, their actions will likely stem from the opinions and assessments being tossed around. For example, if the consensus among Teri's managers was that store owners would resist the notion of catering to business folks, they would likely take a more "hard sell" approach. Such an approach guarantees resistance. There is an outside chance that it might succeed, but it would probably become a costly and time-consuming tug-of-war.

Employing future conversations breaks the endless cycle, and in so doing enables you and others to get into action and get results sooner. Pursuing a new possibility tends to create positive action rather than negative reaction. It also ensures that your actions will yield a result beyond what might be reasonably expected. In addition, managing your conversations and shifting to future-domain conversations yields another important long-term benefit: Future-driven action builds and improves relationships.

In our example, Teri's sales team was able to shift the way clients perceived them. As they enrolled customers in the possibility of attracting a vital new customer base, their clients began to see them as *partners* rather than just vendors. By contrast, if they had operated from an opinion that store owners would resist their idea, it would have perpetuated the unspoken conversation among Teri's managers that many store owners were not good business-people. Obviously, no one could build a good relationship with that attitude.

Learning to master the art of conversation not only yields results, it enhances already good relationships and improves poor ones. Since you rarely accomplish any objective on your own, good working relationships are key to long-term sustainable success and the mark of a good leader.

As you have seen, future conversations initially *create* the possibility that drives action. Managing the action that follows is just as important. For that reason, mastering the art of conversation requires that you have ways to initiate and sustain powerful action. That brings us to the next chapter and present-domain conversations.

5

MAKING THINGS
HAPPEN

—

In the relentless effort to accomplish objectives and achieve results, the most common complaint you hear from leaders is that "nothing's happening" or "things aren't moving fast enough." Creating and maintaining action is central to success. As you may suspect by now, the way you speak and listen is the way you create and maintain action, and you will learn how to do that in this chapter. You will learn the fastest and easiest way to get what you want and expect.

The speech act most often associated with the realm of present time is called a *request*. This may not be new information, since you undoubtedly make and receive countless requests every day. However, as in the story in the sidebar on the following page, your requests may be instinctive and mostly unconscious. But any time you can take what you do intuitively and begin doing it intentionally you immediately become more effective.

Ask and Ye Shall Receive

One of my clients began a coaching session grumbling about her current circumstances. "It takes forever to accomplish anything," she lamented. "Changes in this organization are not happening with enough velocity."

I sensed that she might be separating herself from the situation, and possibly blaming others for her predicament since she used the phrase "*this* organization," rather than *my* organization, which was her custom. The first rule of leadership is "take personal responsibility," and I wanted her to do that.

"Why is that happening?" I asked.

Hearing my query as a veiled indictment, she responded defensively. "Are you saying that there's something I'm doing, or should be doing . . . that I'm not?"

To be fair, I suspected that might be the case—but I had never seen her with her management team, so my opinion would only put our coaching conversation into a vicious circle. Instead, I shifted the conversation. "I think the best way to understand why there isn't sufficient velocity within your organization is to observe you and your team in action." We agreed that I would sit in on a staff meeting the next day.

I participated in the next day's staff meeting as an observer only, sitting quietly with a time-domain worksheet like the one described in Chapter 1. As the conversation proceeded, I put a hash mark in the appropriate circle each time someone made a statement. At the conclusion of a rather unpro-

LEARNING TO MAKE PROPER REQUESTS

The process of making a proper request may seem elemental and even mundane, but it might bear review.

A proper request includes three elements:

- Saying *exactly what* you want.
- Saying *exactly when* you want it.
- And saying *exactly who* you want it from.

ductive two-hour meeting the reason for the lack of velocity
was clear.

After the last person left the meeting room my client approached. "See. I told you. Nothing happened," she said.

"That's not entirely true. Something did happen," I
replied. "What was it?"

My client was puzzled. "All that happened was that we
decided to have another meeting. Is that what you mean?"
she said.

"That's it. How did that happen?" I asked.

"How did the meeting happen?" She paused in thought.
"I just asked everyone to look at their calendars to see if they
could meet tomorrow."

"Right. And what do you call what you did?" I inquired.

"I don't know. Asking?" she reflected.

"It's called a request. You made a request," I noted. "How
many *other* requests did you or other people make during
that meeting?"

After a thoughtful pause my client responded, "Not many."

"Not any," I added, showing her and explaining about
the hash marks in the three circles. Her request for another
meeting showed up as the one lone hash mark in the present
domain.

The primary speech act that creates action and increases
velocity is the request. The more requests, the more action
and change. The more unreasonable the requests, the
greater the change. Indeed, you might say that the function
of a leader is to make unreasonable requests.

The operative word is *exactly*. The less precise you are in
making your requests, the greater the chance you will not
get what you want or expect.

When we don't get what we want, we usually blame
someone else, but the majority of the time, it's our fault.
Most requests we make and receive are vague and unclear.
It's a wonder we ever get what we want.

Let's say you just completed a lengthy problem-solving
discussion with a small group of people. You might say,
"Let's try to capture and summarize this discussion in

some way. Will one of you develop a report that I can send on to the executive council?" Heads nod. As you leave the meeting room, you feel confident that a report is forthcoming. However, given the nature of your request, it is highly likely you will be disappointed.

The request, "Will one of you develop a report that I can send on to the executive council?" was lacking on every count:

- It did not state *exactly who* was responsible. You may want everyone's input on the report, but most requests you make should have a single point of accountability, even if it's someone to lead a team effort.
- The request did not state *exactly what* you wanted. The term "report" means different things to different people. You might be expecting a 2- or 3-page outline; others might assume a 20-page narrative.
- Finally, the request did not state *exactly when* you wanted the report.

It would border on a miracle if you were to get the report you want, when you want it, given this poor request. Of course, this example was extreme because it was lacking all three elements of a proper request. Most of the time, the requests you make and receive may be lacking one or two of the elements. Even partially effective requests run the risk of not generating the results a leader wants and needs.

Your requests don't need to be uttered in a mechanical formula—that is, you don't have to say, "Mary, please develop and write a three- to five-page report summarizing the three action items coming out of this meeting, and get it to me by five o'clock tomorrow." There is nothing wrong with such a request, but you may feel uncomfortable speaking that way, particularly to people you work with on a regular basis.

You should make requests in a manner that is comfortable and natural. Just be sure to cover the three essential elements. You might say, "Mary, I noticed you were taking good notes during this meeting. Would you take the lead, work with your colleagues here, and summarize the three action items we came up with today? Nothing fancy, three to five pages will do. And can you get it to me by the end of the day tomorrow . . . say by five o'clock?"

Making a request in a manner that fits your style and working relationship is smart and easy to do. Just include exactly what, exactly when, and exactly who. Speaking in this manner will let you generate the action you want. However, there is one other distinction you need in order to create and maintain action—a proper response.

GETTING PROPER REPLIES

It may be all too obvious, but making a request is only half of the conversation that creates action. The other half has to do with getting a valid or proper response. As with requests, responses we get and give may be a little sloppy. Unfortunately, an imprecise reply to a request all but invalidates that request.

There are only four proper replies or responses to a request.

- Accept
- Decline
- Counteroffer
- Promise to reply later

If you let someone give you anything except one of these responses, there is a good chance that the action you want and need will not be forthcoming.

Accept means that the individual or individuals you are making your request to agree to take the action you have described in your request, on the terms you stated.

Decline means just the opposite. The person or persons to whom you have made your request say no. (This is okay. If someone has valid reasons for not doing what you want, you need to know about it and adjust either the request or the target—or address their reasons if you have both the power and the need to do so. But don't attack someone for refusing; that will only lead to waffling and disguising intended noncompliance in the future.)

A *counteroffer* is a reply in which some aspect or element of your request is changed or modified. For example, "I can't have the report done by five o'clock tomorrow, but I could get it to you by the end of the following day." This response may or may not be acceptable to you, and thus such a counteroffer often involves a brief negotiation process. If you are clear about your conditions for satisfaction (which will be explored in a moment), these negotiations are usually quick and end up creating the action and activity you desire.

A *promise to reply later* effectively puts the response on hold to give someone time to consider your request, and possibly to gather more information to aid in making a decision. For example, "I can't give you a definite answer now, but I'll let you know in an hour." It is important that any delaying tactic state *exactly when* you can expect the reply. If a reply lacks a specific time, it becomes what might be called a *nonresponse*.

DEALING WITH NONRESPONSES

You will almost always get some type of response to your requests. However, not every reply, as positive as it may seem, will lead to action. Many replies you will get—and accept, if you're not careful—are actually vague nonresponses. For example:

- I'll think about it.
- I'll look into that.

- I'll try.
- That's a great idea.
- As soon as I can get to it.
- That's outside my control, but I'll see what I can do.
- I'll make it a priority.
- I'll see what my boss says.

The list of nonresponses is nearly infinite and oftentimes ingenious. We have all become experts at dodging requests we can't or don't want to handle. Nonresponses like, "I'll see what I can do," are insidious because they imply acceptance. Indeed, the person making such a statement might have every intention of granting your request, but you cannot be certain until you get one of the four proper replies to a request.

If you get a nonresponse, it's easy to follow up and get a committed reply. For example, if someone says, "I'll see what I can do," just add, "Does that mean you will do it?" If you get a yes, you have acceptance. If you get another nonresponse, you will have to continue the conversation until you get a proper response. As you are learning, *mastering the art of conversation takes not only awareness, distinctions, and conversational tools, it takes gracious persistence.* You must learn to be persistent without being aggressive or demanding. Indeed, the fear of being perceived as a demanding SOB is one barrier to making proper requests and demanding proper replies, but there are many other barriers as well.

OVERCOMING THE BARRIERS TO MAKING REQUESTS

Why don't we make requests? Why accept nonresponses? There are as many reasons as there are persons and personalities. One obvious concern is that people will say no or feel that you're pushy. However, the primary reason

Why Didn't You Say So?

Part of the deal I have with my coaching clients is that they can call me any time they need coaching or help of any kind. On one particular day, one of my clients, who was leading a special task team, called with an urgent request.

"Can you make it to a meeting my team is having this Thursday?" he asked.

After consulting my calendar, I replied, "No. Sorry, I can't make it Thursday."

There was a long pause at the other end. "Maybe I can change the meeting. I'll get back to you," my client said, and hung up.

A few hours later he called again. "How about Friday afternoon? Can you make a meeting Friday afternoon?"

"No, that won't work either," I said apologetically. I could tell my client was distraught, and I wanted to help. However, I wanted him to come to grips with a behavior that I had observed was causing him problems now and in the past. I remained silent.

"Look, I've got a problem with two of my people on the team. They're constantly bickering and their infighting wastes time and is beginning to divide the team into warring camps."

"That's not good," I said.

Getting somewhat angry now, my client added, "I want you to help me do something about this situation. Can you?"

Finally, my client made a real request. "Why didn't you ask me that the first time you called?" I replied. "I think I can help you."

Before addressing his concern, I noted that making indirect requests rather than asking for what he really wanted was something that was causing him problems. He asked me to attend a meeting, but what he really wanted was help in resolving an interpersonal dispute between two teammates.

people don't get what they want is that they don't *know* what they want—not exactly. You may be able to formulate a request, but oftentimes the thing or action you are requesting is what I like to call *once removed* from what you really want.

Sometimes we make once-removed or indirect requests because we're afraid of asking for what we really want or we're afraid our request will be declined. Or maybe we don't want to make waves. However, most of the time, making indirect requests is the result of not being clear about what we want. As a result, our requests are vague and ambiguous. For example, you might ask the boss "how do you think things are going?" when what you really want is feedback about the task you just completed.

A good question to ask yourself before you make a request is, "What do I want to happen or stop happening as a result of what I'm about to say?" The answer to that question will help you develop a clearer and more precise request. In this case, what you want is an assessment of your performance by your boss. What you're likely to get if you ask how things are going is a general summary of your boss's problems. So you should ask straight out for the evaluation and acknowledgment you desire. For example, "If you have a moment now, I'd like your assessment of the project." Assuming a proper reply, this will get you what you want.

Making clear requests and getting proper replies is the best way to create action. In addition, spending a little more time analyzing and developing proper requests has an additional benefit. It gets you in touch with your conditions for satisfaction.

KNOWING YOUR CONDITIONS OF SATISFACTION

As you formulate proper requests, your deeper wants and needs reveal themselves. Suppose you need someone to complete a report so you can get it to your boss. However, as you prepare to make your request, you recall that the boss is going out of town tomorrow and you would like him to be able to review it while he travels. This means that any changes in the report would have to be made quickly and the report will probably have to be hand-carried to the boss. So as conditions for satisfaction surface, your request becomes clearer and more specific. In addition, you become better prepared to negotiate if and when you get a counteroffer in response to your request.

For example, if you ask a person to make changes in the report before lunch and they counter with, "I can't do it before lunch, but maybe by the end of the day," your conditions of satisfaction will not be met. The end of the day will be too late. So offers and counteroffers will have to continue until you got a committed response that meets all your conditions for satisfaction. If you are having difficulty getting acceptance, you might consider using another speech act to facilitate action.

MAKING PROMISES

A promise, which is similar to a request, is a speech act that puts *you* in action. A promise is a request you make of yourself. A proper promise has the same three elements as a request—exactly *what*, exactly *when*, and you are the *who*. For example, the request, "Bob, will you make the changes we talked about in this report before lunch today?" becomes "I will make the changes we talked about in this report before lunch today," as a promise.

Requests and promises are the only two speech acts that will definitely create action. And *requests become more powerful and compelling when they are coupled with promises*. For example, "If you will make the changes in this report before lunch today, I will hand-carry it to Dave this afternoon." The promise that you'll hand-carry the report speaks to your sense of urgency and demonstrates your commitment to the effort. Your promise motivates and compels the individual you're collaborating with to make the changes you requested, by the time you requested them.

Ensuring that action takes place and that activities move at greater speed means including more requests and promises in your conversations. Of course, action alone is no guarantee of future success.

DETERMINING THE SOURCE OF ACTION

Present-realm conversations—requests and promises—generate action. For a manager, action is the game. Managers are expected to keep things moving. Leaders, however, must also be concerned with the *source of action*.

Action driven by opinions, assessments, and interpretations, as you may recall, creates incremental improvement at best. By contrast, action driven by a new possibility creates a fundamentally different future. As a leader, you want future-driven action—action driven by declarations and possibilities. Figure 5-1 illustrates the process.

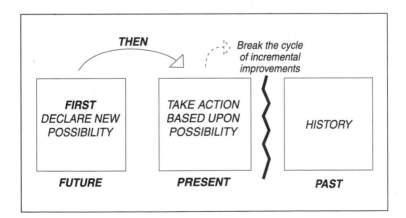

Figure 5-1   Declaring a possibility breaks the endless cycle created by taking action based on opinions or assessments. By taking action on a new possibility, you create a fundamentally different future.

Managing conversations begins with minimizing past conversations and breaking the vicious circle. This break with the past occurs the moment you declare a new possibility. Once sufficient support for the new possibility is established, you can shift the conversation into the domain of action by making requests and promises. The fourth principle you must apply to master leadership conversation is: *Shift the conversation first from the past to the future and then to the present.*

Managing conversations is a one, two, three process. One—stop past conversation. Two—shift into the future. Three—shift into the present.

This all sounds simple, and conceptually it is. However, human nature is such that even the most powerful future-driven action will begin to disintegrate over time and drift into the past. Managing this drift requires constant vigilance and work. This means having the same conversation with the same people, and also sharing the conversation with more people. In most circumstances, the circle of people included in any conversation will grow over time as any new possibility begins to take shape.

Initially, you can use the same set of conversational tools and speech acts to create a new future. You enroll people in the new possibility and put them in action using requests and promises. However, future-focused conversations can lose their power over time. They don't sound as new and exciting the second or third time you hear them. You need additional conversational tools to maintain future-focused action and keep others from getting caught in the drift back into the past. Fortunately, there's a form of conversation ideally suited for this task, and that is what we'll explore in the next chapter.

6

UNLEASHING PEOPLE'S FULL POTENTIAL

Initiating action is one thing; keeping it going is another. This is particularly true when you are leading a large group or organization. Leadership is more than creating possibilities and energizing people. Leaders make things happen. Like all leaders, you will be judged by results— what you accomplish. Unless and until you can create the all-important shift from thinking about something to manifesting it, you will just be a dreamer. This chapter is about making dreams come true.

BRIDGING THE GAP BETWEEN TOMORROW AND TODAY

Exercising your leadership ability requires that you develop and maintain a broad perspective. After all, you are custodian of the future for a group or possibly for an entire organization. To include everyone and reach far

Is *Everyone* Dragging Their Feet?

I had just begun working with a successful executive from a large international company. He and his colleagues had been through a series of powerful leadership development programs during the past year. These intensive workshops had succeeded in creating a new awareness and appreciation for leadership. My client and his colleagues were struggling to make the shift from "command and control" to a more collegial style.

My client's experiences had not only changed his mind, they were showing up in his behavior. He was more patient with those he worked with. He was able to stop micromanaging and start spending more time thinking about the future. All this was good, but when I arrived on the scene, I found an extremely frustrated leader.

"I truly believe that the command and control style is not good for people or the company," he said. "However, I have to be honest. I don't believe I'm as effective as I used to be."

My client and the rest of the executive team had developed a compelling mission and vision nine months earlier. They began a conversation for possibility. They had also made requests during one-to-one meetings with each of their direct

enough into the future, your vision or new possibility has to be broad enough to encompass rapidly changing circumstances. It is this broad perspective that gives a new possibility its potential and power. Ironically, it is also what makes it difficult for others to buy into.

By nature, any totally new possibility you create and promote will at first seem vague and out of reach to others. This is true for two reasons. First, most people's daily work probably requires a narrower focus and perspective than yours does, which makes it hard for people to see the connection between your vision and their work. Second, until a possibility begins to take shape, you don't have all the details and answers to questions that inevitability come reports. "It sounds like you're doing all the right things," I noted.

"You'd think so, wouldn't you? But getting anything done is like pulling teeth," he said. "There's a lot that's bad about the old ways, but we got things done."

"Is *everyone* here dragging their feet?" I responded.

My client was making a common mistake—generalizing. And with a few questions he was able to see that the majority of his folks were in action and wholeheartedly pursuing the vision. Others, for some reason, were not performing up to his expectations. So that's where we focused.

I had already introduced my client to the notion that mastering conversation would give him access to leadership. I built on that awareness. "You declared a new, exciting, and compelling future and shared it with everyone. You put people into action by making requests and promises. Now you're wondering why some people won't buy in and others have to be dragged kicking and screaming."

He nodded in agreement. "You've mastered two key conversations, and that's enough for many people," I assured him. "But some people need more. They need a new conversation—coaching."

up. As you might suspect, both these circumstances tend to disconnect people from your vision or possibility. It's not that they don't see the possibility or like it, but rather that it seems far-fetched, unrealistic, or undoable. This situation makes it difficult to obtain the committed action that you want and need.

It is possible to master future and present conversations and still not be able to create a new future. However, *coaching* bridges the gap between the present and future. Not surprisingly, many organizations don't make use of coaching conversations. Indeed, it seems that most organizations are overmanaged and underled, and coaching is almost totally missing.

CHANGING ORGANIZATIONAL BEHAVIOR

You have undoubtedly noticed that there's been a lot of attention focused on coaching in recent years. It's a hot topic, and for good reason. Coaching changes, focuses, and intensifies human behavior.

Leaders are in a constant struggle to bridge the gap in perspective, as described earlier. How do you initiate and maintain action that will bring your vision to fruition? How do you change and synchronize the behavior of tens, hundreds, or even thousands of people? Those are the questions you have to answer as a leader.

There are many ways to change collective or organizational behavior. Consulting firms have gotten rich by developing and deploying processes and techniques for doing just that. In the seventies, visioning and strategic planning was a powerful means of channeling, focusing, and changing organizational behavior. In the eighties, the focus was on changing organizational "structures" that influence and shape behavior. Processes were "reengineered" and systems redesigned to force changes in behavior. In the nineties, coaching seems to be the change agent of choice.

All the various ways to change human behavior seem to fall into one of two categories, however. You can either change the structures—the processes, systems, policies, procedures, and so on—to force a behavior change and trust that a change in mindset will follow, or you can change mindsets and trust that a behavior change will follow.

For example, if you wanted to make employees at a retail store concentrate more on customers, a *structural approach* to changing behavior might suggest that you rewrite your policies to make it easier to return merchandise or move the sales counters closer to the front of the store to make clerks more accessible to customers when they enter.

If you wanted to go the route of *changing mindsets* to improve customer service, you might ask clerks to participate in customer focus groups to make them more sensitive to customer needs, or shop at competing stores to gain insights and new distinctions for good and bad customer service. Both approaches are valid, and leaders typically employ both methods. However, changing mindsets is a preferable way to change people's behavior because it unleashes the full power and potential of the individual.

Changing behavioral structures tends to limit creativity and flexibility. A friendlier return policy is an improvement, but employees are still bound by a policy. Putting clerks at the front of the store makes them available, but it doesn't ensure that they will greet customers or how they will greet them.

If changing mindsets is the preferred way to change behavior, why then has so much attention and energy gone into changing organizational structures?

As you might suspect, it's because changing mindsets is more difficult. The tools and techniques needed to change mindsets do not seem readily available to the average person. It would appear that changing mindsets requires a set of complex skills typically found in counselors, ministers, and therapists, among others. However, if you take a closer look at any of these "mindset changing professionals" at work you will discover that their primary process and tool is conversation.

Counselors, ministers, and the like have learned to master coaching conversation. You can also. As with past, present, and future conversations, mastery of coaching conversations begins with creating a clear and powerful distinction.

DISTINGUISHING COACHING CONVERSATIONS

Coaching is a conversational tool that creates a climate, environment, and context that gives individuals and groups more confidence and puts them in action on specific goals they are committed to achieving. The operative word in this definition is *they*. When coaching becomes embedded in an organization, you will be able to get away from using control to put people in action and begin motivating them to take action on their own. You'll get all people can give, rather than just what you ask for.

This description might help you understand coaching, but it or any other definition will not enable you to become a good coach. One of the best ways to develop a distinction for coaching is to be coached. And there is little doubt that you have had some powerful and effective coaches in your life—although you may not have thought of them that way.

Think of an individual, past or present, whom you would say has made or is making a difference in your life—helping you see things more clearly and make the world go more smoothly. Chances are, that person is or was a coach. Indeed, that's a great definition of coaching. *A coach is a person who makes a positive difference in someone's life.*

What qualities did this person or coach have that made them effective? Usually they were trusting and trustworthy, they showed genuine concern and love, they looked out for your interests rather than their own.

How did they relate to you? Coaches are typically nonjudgmental and egalitarian.

What did they say and do? Coaches mostly listen and are able to hear at deeper levels. When they did speak they often reflected back what you said, causing you to recognize previously unseen barriers at work in your thinking and your life.

What happened as a result of your association with this person—this coach? You undoubtedly achieved some objective or goal. Indeed, good coaches are judged by the results the people they are coaching achieve.

Most coaching conversations end with the person poised for action. Coaches are not responsible for results, but they are responsible for the individual and team achieving the results. This may seem to be a fine distinction, but it is an important one. A coach focuses on the individual and not on the result. A coach uses conversation to make you aware of limiting assumptions or of previously unseen openings for actions. Creating awareness, which is a key part of coaching, happens in conversation.

HAVING COACHING CONVERSATIONS

While each coaching conversation is different, because every person and situation is unique, there is a basic five-step process that you can use in most circumstances.

• *Step 1: Make sure both you and the individual you are coaching know that you are having a coaching conversation.* In particular, it is vital that the individual being coached listens to what is offered as coaching. Coaching creates expectations that facilitate the process. For example, a coaching conversation carries with it the expectation that action will follow. Designating a conversation as "coaching" differentiates it from idle talk, complaining, or casual advice.

While the easiest way to make it clear that you are offering coaching is to say, "Would you like some coaching?" this might not be possible unless and until the other person knows what coaching is. However, every opening you see for coaching is an opportunity to distinguish coaching for someone else and for your team, department, or organization.

A good way to begin to distinguish coaching is to say what it's *not*. For instance, say, "I'm tempted to give you advice, but instead let me help you gain a different perspective on this issue . . . one that may shed new light and possibly give you more options." When the conversation is complete, you might say, "What just happened is what I call coaching. If it was helpful, feel free to ask for coaching anytime." And the conversation will be helpful if you follow the next four steps.

 • *Step 2: Get the facts, separating fact from interpretation.* This is the most important step. People tend to create problems for themselves or make problems bigger than they are by generalizing and mixing facts with interpretation.

For example, during a speech I recently gave, I noticed two people in the audience get up and leave. The facts were just that—they got up and left. However, I attached an interpretation to them. In this instance, I recall that I felt I probably offended or bored them. I was troubled and upset. At the conclusion of my presentation all I could think about was finding the two people to see what prompted their departure.

I thought about them all day. Fortunately, that evening I had my own biweekly telephone session with my coach. It went something like this:

> *Me:* I got upset today while I was making a presentation.
>
> *Coach:* What happened?
>
> *Me:* About five minutes in, two people near the front got up and left.
>
> *Coach:* And this upset you?
>
> *Me:* I didn't understand why. Were they bored, offended, or what?
>
> *Coach:* Did they say they were bored or offended?
>
> *Me:* No. They didn't say a word. I tried to find them later but—
>
> *Coach:* Did they look bored or offended, or did someone else suggest that they were bored or offended?
>
> *Me:* No.
>
> *Coach:* So what makes you say they were bored or offended?

> *Me:* I don't know. I guess I just assumed the worst.
>
> *Coach:* Maybe they had to go to the bathroom. Do you want to try and guess? Maybe instead, we can focus on why you care, or why you thought the worst. What do you think?

This conversation is not simply a good example of separating fact from interpretation, it also illustrates two related points about coaching: First, that a good coach is coachable; second, that regardless of how expert you are at coaching, you cannot coach yourself because none of us has the perspective needed to see ourselves.

In coaching, as with most other interchange, managing the conversation requires that you fight the drift into the past and shift the talk into the present or future. Separating fact from interpretation helps you make that shift. Oftentimes, the issue or concern that initially prompted the request for coaching disappears or is greatly diminished after step two. This step breaks the endless cycle— action driven from the past. The shift to the future happens next.

• *Step 3: Develop and explore new possibilities.* Once you separate fact from interpretation, new openings for action often pop up. However, even if they don't, you can help generate them. In a way, step three is brainstorming, and it works on two levels.

Step three works on a *content level* by creating a number of viable options and various courses of action. However, it also works on a *psychological level.* Oftentimes, one of the things that creates the breakdown leading to the need for coaching is the feeling that there aren't any options, or at least any desirable options. This usually stops us from taking any action. The process of generating a long list of options, regardless of their quality and viability, is psychologically reassuring and empowering. Therefore, during step three, create as many possibilities and options as you can without evaluating them. That comes next.

• *Step 4: Get some action started.* Ask the person you're coaching to review the list of possible actions and options from step three and pick one or two *they* would like to pursue.

It is critical that the person being coached make the choice. They will often ask your advice. It's tempting, but don't fall into this trap. If you choose or unduly influence the choice, you put yourself in a no-win situation. If your advice doesn't work out, they'll blame you. If it does work, it will take away their sense of accomplishment. They'll feel *you* made it happen. It can also create an unhealthy dependency. Giving advice will tend to make the person being coached feel as though they cannot make good decisions without you. If they ask for your advice, toss it back by simply saying, "I don't know. What do you think?"

Also, in step four, it's a good idea to select more than one option. Taking action on two fronts will usually yield results more quickly. Someone might decide to try one option first, and use the second one as backup, and that's okay too. Once they decide which options or possibilities to pursue, you can close the coaching conversation.

• *Step 5: Bring closure by getting a firm commitment to act and adding a point of accountability.* You should get a committed response when you summarize the action or actions that were identified in step four.

The easiest way to add a point of accountability is to request that they follow up with you to let you know how things went. Of course, you can initiate the follow-up too. Be careful, when adding this point of accountability, that it shows up as genuine care and concern. Coaching is collegial, and should never resemble or become a parent-child type of relationship.

As you will discover, the five steps almost naturally unfold. You are simply facilitating a natural process. As an illustration, here is an annotated account of a recent coaching session with Ted, one of my younger clients.

While you do not want to coach someone who is in a highly emotional state, you will find that most people bring a certain amount of emotion into a coaching session. Such was the case with Ted, a distraught accountant who called late one evening.

- *Step 1: Make sure you and the individual you are coaching know that you are having a coaching conversation.*

  Ted: Sorry to call after hours, but I've got something nagging at me.

  Me: That's fine. That's part of our deal. What's happening?

  Ted: I have this constant nagging feeling that the boss hates me, and I'm afraid it's affecting the way I act.

  Me: It sounds like this has been going on a while, why did you call now?

  Ted: I never had a coach before.

  (With Ted's last statement it was clear he was wanting and expecting coaching. And the fact that he called after hours told me he was upset, so I got down to business.)

- *Step 2: Get the facts, separating fact from interpretation.*

  Me: So, your boss hates you. Is that the truth?

  Ted: Yes.

  Me: Is that the truth?

  Ted: Is there an echo in here? Yeah, the boss hates me. *(I heard anger and hurt and decided to let some of that emotion play out.)*

  Me: *(Knowing it might bring an attack.)* Is that the truth?

  Ted: If you think I'm exaggerating, just say so. Don't play games. *(I caught some flack, but successfully introduced the notion that his interpretation may be off the mark.)*

  Me: *(Trying to get at the facts.)* What makes you say that your boss hates you?

  Ted: Take today. I must have passed him ten times in the hall . . . not once . . . not once did he smile or say "Hi." Canceling my meeting for the umpteenth time was the proverbial last straw.

  Me: Anything else?

  Ted: How much time do you have? What do you think of a boss who hasn't given you a performance review in three years?

  Me: Is your boss a real sociable person? *(It's always best to separate fact from interpretation by asking questions, rather than pointing it out directly. Ideally, you want the person being coached to discover that what they are doing. If you assert that they are making erroneous interpretations, you will more than likely make them defensive and keep them stuck in the endless cycle.*) Does he give high-fives in the halls?

Ted:　He's as sociable as a zombie. (*Sensing his case was beginning to crumble, he moved to other interpretations.*) I've been trying to get a meeting for over two months. The one scheduled today got canceled minutes before. (*Ted went on to regale me, in detail, with his countless and fruitless attempts to have a heart-to-heart conversation with his boss, including efforts to get a performance review.*)

Me:　Is your boss busy?

Ted:　He's on the road most of the time . . . (*Ted paused. His interpretation was loosing its grip.*) Okay, okay, I get it. Maybe he is busy, but that's no excuse.

(*I could tell, through his words and calmer manner, that Ted was beginning to see that his assertion—"the boss hates me"—was shaky. I didn't want to make him feel foolish by pointing that out verbally, so I moved on.*)

- Step 3: Develop and explore new possibilities.

    Me:　You're right. So what are some ways to get a meeting with the boss?

    Ted:　I've tried everything. Today's cancellation was the last straw.

    Me:　What have you tried?

    Ted:　Everything from bribing his secretary to catching him in the john. (*As Ted shared his ingenious but unsuccessful efforts to get a meeting, I could see "the box"—the assumption that kept him from seeing all his options. He assumed the meeting must take place on the job.*)

    Me:　Does the boss eat? I've heard he only eats raw meat, but maybe you could get steak tartare somewhere? (*A little humor rarely hurts—even bad jokes can sometimes turn a viewpoint around.*)

> Ted: You mean like a breakfast or dinner meeting? *(That's all Ted needed to break out of the box. He was off!)* And he plays golf. That's my game!
>
> Me: Three or four hours on a golf cart . . . a few beers along the way. Sounds great to me. *(We went on to generate a few more ideas even though it was clear that Ted really liked the golfing option.)*

- **Step 4: Get some action started.**

> Me: So, what sounds good to you?
>
> Ted: I like the golf outing.
>
> Me: *(Wanting him to have backup plan.)* Anything else?
>
> Ted: Dinner would be nice, too. Maybe golf and dinner? *(I could hear and feel the energy flowing back into Ted. He was ready to go, so I moved on quickly.)*

- **Step 5: Bring closure by getting a firm commitment to act and adding a point of accountability.**

> Me: So, what are you going to do now?
>
> Ted: First see if I can get a Saturday or Sunday tee time. Then check with the boss.
>
> Me: You're going to do that when?
>
> Ted: First thing in the morning.
>
> Me: *(Adding the point of accountability.)* Good, call me today or tomorrow if it doesn't work out, otherwise call me Monday or Tuesday to let me know how the golf game or dinner went. Will you do that?
>
> Ted: Sure.
>
> Me: You've come up with some great ideas. Thanks for calling.
>
> Ted: Thanks for listening.

This five-step coaching process is simple, but mastering it takes time and practice. The best way to become an effective coach is to coach and be coached. Often that requires that you overcome the natural fear that comes up when you consider having a coaching conversation.

Overcoming Fear of Coaching

There seem to be three primary reasons people are reticent to offer coaching:

- They don't have a clear distinction for coaching.
- They don't understand the basic objective and process involved in coaching.
- They fear failure.

This last reason may be the biggest barrier to coaching. The fear that somehow you might screw up and make things worse or make yourself look incompetent can be a powerful deterrent. However, as you begin to explore and practice coaching you will undoubtedly become aware of a powerful ally—intention.

Intention is the foundation for all conversations. Intention is the driver or underlying message. It's not necessary to write a chapter about intention because it will manifest automatically. You cannot create it or hide it. If you think you can, you're kidding yourself. Even a child can detect and translate intention. Indeed, children may be better equipped to understand the intention behind communication than adults, who tend to focus more on the content.

If you doubt the power of intention, think for a moment about how you communicate to a dog, cat, or other pet. Obviously, it's not your words as much as your intention, your overall demeanor, that gets your message across. When you speak and listen you automatically communicate your intention through the tone of your voice, your pace, the way you hold your eyes, your body language, word choice, and so on. You use tens or maybe hundreds of behavioral signals to transmit your intention. You do this unconsciously and automatically.

If you want to try an interesting experiment, create a mismatch between your intention and your words. Take a group of friends who are trying to decide where to go for lunch, for example. If someone makes a suggestion you really don't like say, "That sounds great." Watch the reaction you get. When your words conflict with your intention people will probe and ask questions to reconcile the dissonance in your communication. "Are you sure . . . 'cause we can go anywhere you want," they might respond. They will continue this tactful interrogation until your words and intention are the same. If they are eager to please you, they might immediately suggest other options. That's because most people have learned to trust the intention rather than the words being communicated.

We have all learned to trust intention because it is natural and honest. And it is this innate trust of intention that makes even the most unskilled coach powerful and effective.

When your intention to help another person is clear, your coaching conversations will have the desired effect, regardless of the process or words you use. The person you are coaching will hear your care and concern and eagerly participate in the conversation. And in the end, it's how your message is received that is important. This brings up the next big subject with regard to conversation—listening.

7

THE BETTER HALF OF CONVERSATION

When we use the term *conversation*, speaking is what usually comes to mind first. However, speaking is only part of a conversation, and not the biggest part. In the end, what makes a difference is what is heard, accepted, and internalized, not what is said.

This chapter will give you a new distinction, insight, awareness, and appreciation for the power of *listening*, that is, for the power of creatively and actively absorbing what people say. Learning to manage your listening and that of others unleashes the power of your speaking. When you treat listening with the same care and concern you put into speaking, your conversations will have the influence and effect you want.

Listening is an internal process. You are not privy to how other leaders listen. Consequently, listening is often overlooked in leadership development, even though it may be the most important leadership skill. Mastering it will make a big difference in your life and work.

CONTROLLING THE "LITTLE CRITIC" INSIDE YOU

Stop reading for a moment and listen to your *little* voice—the one inside your head. If you are wondering what I mean, I mean the voice that's saying, "What little voice? I don't have a little voice"—that one. We all have a little voice that is chattering away all the time.

You might believe this little voice is your mind in the process of thinking. But is it? There may be some creative thought mixed in, but the conversation going on inside you—your little voice—is not really thinking. Indeed, if you pay attention, you will notice that it's mostly judging, evaluating, and criticizing. You might think of your little voice as the "little critic" since it comments on everything—what others say and well as your own thoughts. It's doing a play-by-play commentary on everything that happens.

Your little voice is not bad, indeed it is helpful in several ways. However, if you don't manage it, it can cause as many problems for you as the things you say out loud.

MANAGING YOUR LISTENING

The notion of managing your listening may seem even more strange than managing your speaking, but mastering the art of listening will transform not only your conversations but your life.

You are mostly unaware of the way you listen, because your listening process or mechanism is automatic. You don't engage your little voice, it's always present. You may be able to quiet the little critic, but you can never turn it off completely. And if you practice quieting it, or have ever tried to meditate, you understand how difficult it is to manage the chatterbox in your head.

So the bad news is, you can't turn off your little voice.
The good news is that through awareness and practice you
can *manage* it. Why manage it? Because your little voice,
while helpful in some ways, makes it nearly impossible to
shift your speaking and drive your actions from the present or future. Your little voice speaks from the past.

Think about it. Your little voice is judging, evaluating, interpreting, advising, criticizing. These speech acts belong
in the *past*. When you judge something, on what do you
base your judgment? Usually it involves a comparison with
what already exists, or what has already happened.

Each day we make thousands of decisions, most of them
small and inconsequential. Should I wear my red jacket
today? Should I finish the report or go to lunch with the
gang? Should I start the meeting now? If we stopped to
analyze and evaluate each of these decisions, we wouldn't
get much done in a day. We need to make quick snap decisions most of the time, since the majority of the decisions we make have relatively little significance or
consequence. However, some decisions are more important than others. This is where managing your listening
comes in.

Because your automatic way of listening is based in the
past, it makes it impossible or difficult for you to shift
conversations into the future and present. The moment
any new possibility is offered, as when someone says,
"What if we try something new?" automatic listening kicks
in. "We can't do that *because*—" is the mantra of the little
voice. It kicks in with reasons, excuses, stories, predictions,
evaluations, and the like, all based on past events. This
way of listening is not just something that happens
from time to time. It is the normal, ongoing human listening process.

So, if your listening is automatic, and you can't shut off
your little voice, how do you manage it? The same way you
manage your speaking—through awareness and by creating new, more powerful distinctions for listening.

Dealing with Your Listening Filters

Our automatic way of listening is *reactive.* That is, our little voice reacts to what we think and hear. The first step in managing and shifting your listening is to catch yourself listening reactively. As with your speaking, awareness is the first step in managing your listening. Developing distinctions for reactive listening will help you do this. Let's create a distinction for reactive listening by identifying some of the ways you listen.

You listen through a variety of what might be called reactive filters. For example, "I already know this," is a common type of reactive listening. It acts like a filter because, when you listen this way, what mostly gets through is information you already know. In other words, your listening is focused on the information that validates your thinking. What you filter out is the new information; the stuff you don't know. No doubt, when the conversation is completed, you will leave it knowing you were "right," but you pay a dear price for this. You remain stuck in the past. You miss out on the information you didn't know, information that might have contributed to new possibilities, growth, and development.

There are hundreds if not thousands of reactive listening filters like these:

- What's the point?
- This is like—
- What's wrong or missing?
- Where's this going?
- What's in this for me?
- Will this work?

Of course, the ultimate filter drops in place when you mentally check out—when you're "out to lunch," as the saying goes. But even out-to-lunch listening or nonlistening can be managed. To understand how, let's look at what happens when you're out to lunch.

Mastering the Listening Process

When someone else is speaking and your mind drifts off
the subject, what happens? The process is simple.

1. You're listening, and then your mind and attention
   begin to wander.
2. After a while, you catch yourself out to lunch—not
   paying attention.
3. You check in to see what is going on.
4. You make a quick decision whether or not to listen.
   And if you do—
5. You begin listening again.

However, there is a big difference between the way you
were initially listening and the way you listen after you
catch yourself. After you check in, you will usually begin
listening more intensely and effectively. Maybe you are
embarrassed, or maybe you want to see if you missed anything important. The point is, whenever you manage your
listening, you usually end up with more powerful and
effective listening.

This process of catching yourself, checking in, and ultimately listening more intensely when you've been out to
lunch is a normal, natural listening management process.
It is intuitive and unconscious. However, this same listening management process can be employed consciously
and intentionally. You can manage your reactive listening
by consciously identifying how you are listening, stopping
yourself from listening reactively, and starting to listen
more powerfully—affirmatively.

Using Affirmative Listening

What I call *affirmative* listening is not the same as *active* listening, which you may have learned about in school or in
a training class. Affirmative listening is not about making

eye contact, nodding, asking questions, and occasionally parroting what you're hearing. You can do all that while you're out to lunch, with a bit of practice.

While reactive listening can be thought of as *listening to*, affirmative listening is *listening for*—listening for possibility. If it helps, you can invent affirmative filters. Instead of listening through "I already know this," try listening through "I don't know this." Or listen for new ideas, or how you are alike, for ways to partner and collaborate, for shared values you didn't expect to find. Create and use whatever affirmative filters enable you to hear everything being spoken.

Affirmative listening connects you to others, rather than separating you. It enables you to break the endless cycle, move beyond the status quo, and—most important—grasp and act on new possibilities. Indeed, as shown in Figure 7-1, affirmative listening not only enables you to hear every word, it enables you to hear more than what people say.

Without the ability to listen affirmatively, you're likely to find much of the rest of the advice in this book useless. Affirmative listening is what makes it possible for you to

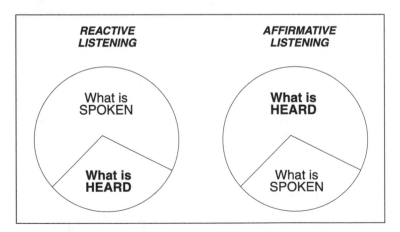

Figure 7-1 Affirmative listening enables you to hear *more* than what is spoken.

create and speak possibility. It starts in your own mind; you need to listen affirmatively to your own thoughts. Otherwise, the moment a really new idea comes to you, your little voice will kick in—judging it, diminishing it, probably shooting it down. If you don't catch yourself, your ideas—and the possibilities they hold—will be gone forever.

This is true not only of ideas and possibilities but of people as well. As a leader, if you don't listen to others affirmatively, you will miss whatever possibilities they have to share, and you'll have lousy relationships to boot. Take jerks, for example. You undoubtedly work with one or two jerks. Picture one of them speaking now. . . .

He's probably saying something stupid, because that's what jerks do. They speak "jerkese," which (of course) you and I don't understand, so we don't listen. And that's the point. There's a reactive listening filter you might call "the jerk filter." All that comes through is the stuff that confirms your assessment. As a consequence, you're missing any good stuff that might be there. And not just from jerks.

Make a list of the people you work with every day. Then go through the list to determine what you personally think of each one—what labels you have attached to them. Based on your assessment, how do you listen to them—more important, *do* you listen to them? As an exercise, try to spend a whole day listening—really listening, as though you'd just caught yourself mentally out to lunch while an important customer was talking—to everyone who talks to you. You know she's an airhead. You know he's a jerk. You can't bear that stutter. But everybody plays the lead in their own personal drama, and everybody eventually has something to say that's worth hearing—and you won't hear it if you don't listen.

As a leader, if you're going for bold new possibilities, you need to tap every resource at your disposal. The most valuable resources are the ideas, suggestions, innovations, and creativity of your people. Many great ideas, insightful suggestions, and breakthrough innovations are lost in listening—yours and that of others. So before you can manage and shift conversations with others, you must make the shift yourself. But what about others? How do you manage other people's listening?

MANAGING AND SHAPING OTHER PEOPLE'S LISTENING

While it's even more difficult to manage and shape the way other people listen than to keep your own little voice in order, it is possible. In fact, you do it all the time. It's called couching. Oftentimes when you expect an adverse or unusual response to something you intend to say, you create a more positive context by offering preliminary comments. For example, if you wanted to offer an idea that is likely to sound weird, you might precede your suggestion by saying, "You may think this idea is a bit strange, but I'd ask you to think about it before responding."

What you are actually doing when you couch is tapping into other people's listening—the listening you anticipate or expect. You are making an instinctive guess as to what their little voice is saying. And, by bringing that little voice out into the open, you disempower or negate it.

You see, one of the things that makes that little voice so powerful is the fact that what it says tends to slide by without examination. Once you call attention to that internal conversation, the conscious mind immediately stops to see if the patter makes sense. That diminishes some of the power of the little voice even when its observations seem apt to the current situation.

When you drop a stack of papers, you might say, "You'd think I was clumsy judging from this juggling act." And suddenly you seem less clumsy. Or when you're late for an appointment, you might say, "Sorry I kept you waiting. It was rude of me"—and that makes it easier for others to forget and forgive. It's as though you put words to what someone else is thinking before they do, and that makes it your idea instead of theirs—and thus easier for them to reject. Most of the time, you use couching defensively and reactively. However, you can use it proactively to shape and manage other people's listening.

Recalling that the little voice and most conversations tend to get stuck in the past, you can and often should precede any declarations with affirmative and reactive couching. For example, "This idea may sound strange at first, but it has the potential to put us in the top ten." First you disempower their little voice by saying, "This might sound strange at first." Then you associate what you are about to say with something positive: "It has the potential to put us in the top ten."

Affirmative couching is something you probably do intuitively. However, as was pointed out earlier, any time you can take what you do intuitively and do it consciously and intentionally, you become more effective. The fifth conversational principle is: *Manage your listening and that of others by couching and by substituting proactive for reactive listening.* In other words, manage your listening and that of others. The two go together, as one of my long-time coaching clients was reminded in a recent conversation.

Laura worked for a large nonprofit organization. I coached her for more than a year. As often happens, our relationship became more collegial as time went on and she only called occasionally. This time it was before a critical presentation she was about to make.

Laura: This is the big one. The presentation is prepared and ready to go and I thought I'd better prepare myself.

Me: What are your concerns?

Laura: I'm proposing something pretty radical and I could use some help figuring out the best way to couch it—so I don't go down in flames.

(I could see that Laura was focused on the wrong thing and probably headed for trouble.)

Me: So you are worried about how they'll be listening to you?

Laura: Right. Any ideas?

Me: I'm not sure how they will be listening to you, but it's pretty clear to me how you're listening to them.

Laura: How's that?

Me: You tell me.

Laura: I think they're going to have trouble with what I'm going to propose.

Me: You know your people better than I do— maybe too well, so I won't take issue with your assessment. But let me ask you this. . . . If you feel that they won't like your ideas, and they are going to shoot you down, how will that make you behave?

Laura: Let's see. I'm bound to be a little defensive. I'll probably push pretty hard.

Me: What about how you feel about each of them personally.

Laura: Many of them are short-sighted and stuck in the past, you know . . . the way we've always done it.

Me: Do you think your attitude might show up? And, if so, how?

Laura: I may appear . . . I may be condescending at times, maybe a bit arrogant.

Me: Let's stop here. Given what you just told me, about being defensive, pushy, condescending, and arrogant, how do you think they will react?

Laura: They'll turn me off.

> *Me:* So your suspicions were right after all. They might shoot you down—but don't give them the bullets to do it.

Couching, or speaking into other people's listening, is an effective way to shape and manage other people's listening. But keep in mind that you only have a limited ability to influence and shape other people's listening. Meanwhile, you have total control over your own listening, and there's more power in that than you can imagine. Coupled with your new appreciation for speaking, you are now equipped with the *core* distinctions needed to master leadership conversation. However, there are a few more conversational distinctions that will aid you as you apply these new concepts and processes in your daily work.

8

MORE CONVERSATIONAL TOOLS

———

By now you are beginning to understand how and why distinctions are the source of mastery. Distinctions create a deep, ingrained awareness that automatically changes the way you think and act. Distinguishing speaking and listening as reflecting the past, present, or future enables you to identify and shift the overall flow of conversations. Distinguishing the various speech acts enables you to consciously speak in a way that enables you to create possibility, action, and relationship. With each new distinction comes new power and effectiveness. It's worth repeating: The more distinctions you have, the more masterful you become.

Building on your ability to distinguish, this chapter will help you identify several other conversational tools you will need once you begin to create a new future for your yourself and your business. Some of these conversational tools are probably familiar to you. Even so, redistinguishing them and putting them in the context of leadership conversations will make them more useful.

CREATING AND INVENTING DISTINCTIONS

A good way to create distinctions is to build on the ones you already have or borrow distinctions created by other people. You might recall Joe, who created some useful distinctions for his customers' complaints. Rather than seeing all complaints as a past conversation that makes no difference, he distinguished *recreational complaining* and *complaining for action*. He had other distinctions as well, such as *complaining for appreciation* and *complaining for help*.

Careful observation might reveal that oftentimes people complain about unsatisfactory circumstances that they are coping with successfully. For example, have you ever come back from a difficult presentation to a top-level group complaining about the "idiots" you "finally convinced" to support your idea or efforts? What would that sound like to someone who was really listening? Maybe something like, "I didn't think I could pull it off at first, but somehow I got through and made them see I was right." What on the surface may sound like an attack and complaint about the quality of leadership is actually a hidden request for acknowledgment. The desired response is not, "You're right, they are a band of idiots," but rather, "Wow, you're fantastic."

Likewise you might occasionally hear an individual complaining, not so much about their circumstances, but about *their ability* to cope with those circumstances. You might hear someone say, for example, "Those guys like to shoot from the hip and ask questions later. It's a great presentation, but it may not be enough." That may sound like a complaint about management style, but it's really a request for help and coaching.

Of course, you can create distinctions for anything from appraisals to zingers. I use complaining here because it's something everyone can relate to. People seem to be an endless source of complaints. And, as a leader, if your only distinction for complaining is "talk that doesn't make a difference," you will be missing out on many opportunities to motivate people and put them in action. If you don't hear *recreational complaining*, you are missing out on having some fun with your coworkers. If you don't hear *complaining for action* or *complaining for help*, you will be missing out on an opportunity to coach and put people in action. If you don't hear *complaining for appreciation*, you will miss an opportunity to acknowledge and motivate someone who shares your commitment.

As noted earlier, it really doesn't matter whether you create your own distinctions or acquire them from others. In general, the more distinctions you have, and the more areas you have them in, the more effective you will be. Of course, some distinctions are more useful in a business arena than others. And, with that in mind, let's explore three new distinctions for conversation that will support and enhance your leadership ability—dialogue, enrollment, and completing the past.

The "Learning" Conversation

Dialogue is often used interchangeably with discussion— as in "Let's have a dialogue." However, it's a special kind of conversation originally distinguished by the ancient Greeks. You may be familiar with the dialogues of Plato. Having and using a distinction for dialogue will enable you to facilitate a critical business process—learning.

If you accept the notion that the ultimate benefit of leadership is long-term sustainable growth, then you can appreciate the role learning plays in that process. Growth is a function of learning. You can probably recall an experience or incident of which you can say, "I grew as a result of that." Growth of all kinds, particularly personal growth, results from new knowledge—and not just any knowledge.

One useful way to distinguish the domain of knowledge is to categorize it in one of three ways as sketched in Figure 8-1. There are a number of things you know. Then there are those things you don't know—and you know you don't know them. However, you have access to them because you can read a book, go to a training class, or seek expert advice. Finally, there is the third kind of knowledge—things you-don't-know-you-don't-know. This is the biggest category and the one most difficult to gain access to.

Typically you stumble into the domain of what-you-don't-know-you-don't-know. You might say, you learn unintentionally. This often happens, for example, when you work in a country or culture strange to you. A few years ago, I thought I knew a lot about coaching. I also thought my coaching techniques were universally applicable— then I began to teach and coach in Russia. I found out the hard way about the influence and power of culture on coaching. Until then, my approach to coaching was based on the notion of taking personal responsibility for

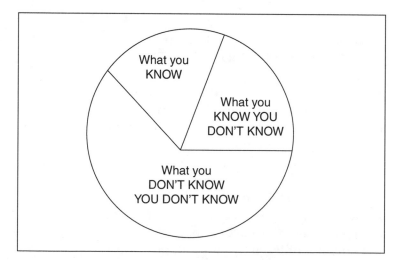

Figure 8-1   The three kinds of possible knowledge: What-you-don't-know-you-don't-know is where leadership development and personal growth reside.

circumstances. I discovered that the idea of personal responsibility is vague and almost missing for most Russian people. For them, responsibility is something that is shared. What I didn't-know-I-didn't-know was that a sense of personal responsibility is not innate but cultural.

However, you don't have to wait for an accident to bring you face to face with the third domain of knowledge. You can create a context or process that forces you to confront what-you-don't-know-you-don't-know.

Ropes courses—planned experiences where you and others do things like climb a wall or cross a river—are physical challenges intended to make you aware of what you don't know about yourself and the way you relate to others. Taking on the challenge of walking a log 20 feet over a raging river has a tendency to bring out the best and worst in you. However, the physical event is only a catalyst for the process that is *really* responsible for learning. The debriefing that follows the event or events is where you discover what you-didn't-know-you-didn't-know. This follow-up conversation is an example of dialogue between a ropes course guide and the client who just finished balancing on a 20-foot-high log.

Guide: Well done. You did it.

Client: I probably wouldn't have if my teammates weren't here.

Guide: What do you mean?

Client: I didn't want to let 'em down.

Guide: I can understand that. Any other reasons why your teammates' presence made a difference?

Client: I can do anything they can do. I just wanted them to know that too.

Guide: Is that something they need to know?

Client: I think so. Some of them think they're better than me.

Guide: Are they?

Client:	No. Hell, I'm better.
Guide:	*(Intentionally silent)*
Client:	That's a heck of thing to say . . . you know . . . when we're out here working on teamwork and all.
Guide:	Are you embarrassed?
Client:	Yeah, a little. But deep down it's how I feel.
Guide:	How might that feeling impact your relationships on the team?
Client:	It would explain a lot about the alienation I experience.
Guide:	And maybe the alienation they experience too?
Client:	Yeah, I never thought about that.

A dialogue is a conversational inquiry. It looks into an area or subject in order to gain greater understanding. The only objective is awareness and new knowledge leading to growth and development.

By contrast, most conversations—particularly those in a business or professional environment—are *discussions* rather than dialogues. Without getting into semantics, you may recall from Chapter 1 that the word *discussion* comes from the Latin *discutere,* which means to take apart. Discussion is a form of conversation based on the Newtonian idea that you can best understand something by dissecting it—that you can understand the whole by revealing its parts. This approach is not without merit. Indeed, it is the basis for much of what we call modern science. Not surprisingly, discussion is the primary conversational form in business, and it's the right form to use when you want to solve problems. However, if you want to learn and develop yourself or your organization, you need something different.

Dialogue is the conversational form to use when you want to create new knowledge—when you want to delve into the domain of what-you-don't-know-you-don't-know. Learning to conduct and facilitate dialogues is a critical leadership tool. The process is simple, but putting it into practice is not.

CONDUCTING A DIALOGUE

Despite the "twoness" of the word, dialogues usually involve groups of people. If you are participating in a dialogue, the process is essentially one of sharing experiences, ideas, and awareness. What one person shares may spark other memories and experiences, and in this way dialogue can be a kind of building process. However, much of the time, what is shared does not directly relate to prior observations and comments. The building process inherent in dialogue is simply the accumulation of human knowledge and understanding. In some respects, it is the antithesis of discussion. Instead of taking an idea, event, or experience apart to understand it, dialogue is the accumulation of parts—insights, ideas, observations, awareness, and so on—leading to understanding. Each idea or experience shared provides a different perspective on the subject or topic. Having a wide variety of perspectives on a topic or issue creates a more reliable and accurate understanding. That's the one and only objective of dialogue—better understanding.

The dialogue process typically begins with someone stating the topic of the dialogue. Ideally, this should be relatively broad—in most cases, the broader the topic the better. For example, a dialogue on the topic of relationships would engender more learning than one focused on friendship. The narrower the subject, the more limited the dialogue will be. In general, the dialogue process works best when there are few limitations. For that reason, there are few rules, but there are some helpful guidelines.

When you participate in a dialogue:

- Draw on your personal experience, but don't moralize.
- Share your beliefs and understanding, but don't try to convince others.
- Try on new ideas and ways of thinking.
- Don't analyze or judge what others say.
- Look into all areas of your life for understanding.
- Speak from your heart.

As a dialogue proceeds, try to maintain these five processes within yourself:

1. A *deep, generative listening* that involves listening for what a person feels and is committed to, and not just what they say.
2. The *suspension of assumptions.* You don't necessarily give up your assumptions about the world, but you hold them back or put them aside so you might gain a different perspective.
3. A *spirit of inquiry* about yourself and others. The objective is not to definitely know or define something, but to see it in all its dimensions.
4. *Respect* for yourself, other participants, and the dialogue process.
5. *Internal awareness*—the ability to notice and observe your own reactions.

This last point is critical. Any time you notice a physical reaction to something being said, or something you are thinking, it's an indicator that you have probably come up against one of your assumptions, beliefs, or values. A "body response" beckons you to reexamine your worldview, your personal paradigm—what we referred to earlier as "your box."

The dialogue process will help you grow beyond your box. That's the good news. The bad news is, you're just in a new box. But that's okay because it's a bigger box. There's room for more possibility. In this way, dialogue complements declarations, the primary speech act associated with creating a new future. Dialogue enlarges and broadens individual and collective perspectives and ultimately enables you and others to see and declare new possibilities.

To give you a better feel for dialogue, what follows is an excerpt from an ongoing dialogue on leadership I've been holding with two colleagues. This segment turned out to be a great learning experience for me.

Me: It seems that leadership development is more intrinsic than extrinsic. It's like trying to cultivate a garden under a blanket.

A: I like that metaphor because it reveals a trap we can fall into—the tendency for us to develop someone else.

Me: Say more.

A: I know each person must take charge of their own development, but I oftentimes act as though I can do it for them.

B: Yes, and this can create unrealistic expectations on everyone's part.

Me: How would you change the gardening metaphor?

B: I give *them* the hoe, or cultivator, for starters.

A: Yes, and I was just struck with the realization that, if we can't really see what's going on under the blanket, how can we expect others to see it?

Me: We see it . . . others see it . . . at harvest time.

A: Maybe this metaphor is limiting us. Maybe leadership development is about removing the blanket.

While this dialogue was a bit esoteric, it led to an awareness on my part that, as I work with leaders, I have a tendency to feel I know best. That was revealed in my metaphor where I was holding the hoe and doing the cultivating. What I didn't-know-I-didn't-know (until then), was that my ego was getting in the way of my coaching. This realization marked a turning point for me in my practice. I resolved to make my coaching nondirective. As the saying goes, I go with the flow now.

Dialogue creates a context that fosters the creation of new possibilities—as it did for me with the discovery that my gardening metaphor was limiting my coaching. A declaration focuses attention and energy on the new possibilities that are generated. In my case, I declared that my coaching would be nondirective. Once that possibility was on the table, I went into action. And there is a process and conversation that assisted me, and can assist you, as we shift from possibility into action.

FOSTERING COMMITTED ACTION VIA ENROLLMENT

Declaring a possibility breaks the endless cycle and creates the context whereby action can be driven from the future rather than the past. Making requests based upon this new future will create action . . . if you get a yes. And enrollment is a conversation that will not only help you get that yes, but get whole-hearted action behind it. For there is *action*, and then there is *ACTION!* In other words, we can distinguish levels of action that come in handy for leadership.

There is a kind of action where people go through the motions. Things get done, but there isn't much energy or excitement in the process. With this kind of action, you may get what you ask for, but you will seldom get more. You might label this kind of action *going along*.

Then there is another kind of action that is almost like magic. You may get things started with a request or two, but everyone gets involved quickly, finds out what needs to be done and does it. No one waits to be asked or told. People are enthusiastic and energized. Most of the time you get *more* than you expect or ask for and you achieve results far beyond business as usual. We can label this kind of action *committed action.*

Obviously, you would prefer committed action to going along. Enrollment is a conversation that can help you get it. In essence, enrollment packages your request and keeps you from slipping into the common practice of selling someone on a new idea or possibility.

Typically, when we promote an idea or possibility we generate a long list of reasons why the other person or people should like it and want it. The longer the list the better because the objective is to pile up reasons, overwhelming others with benefits. This approach works, but it often only yields *going along* type action. Enrollment is one alternative to selling.

LEARNING THE ENROLLMENT PROCESS

Enrollment is something you may already be doing intuitively. Distinguishing it further will enable you to do it intentionally and more effectively. There are six steps to the enrollment process. It begins with an introductory or foundation-building step:

- *Step 1: Connect with the person or group you are enrolling on a personal level.* Connect with a person or group at the strongest level—commitment. Focus attention on the ways you are the same. Reflect the things you have in common. In particular, focus on similar commitments you share. For example, it is likely you share a commitment to the group or organization you both belong to. You might also indicate that you come with a request, if that was not clear when you set up this meeting.
- *Step 2: Share your personal commitment, and connect their commitment (identified in step one) with yours.* If the request

you are about to make has to do with adding a new member to your task team, for example, you might talk about your commitment to delivering a breakthrough result that will enable them to more fully realize their commitment. The idea is to focus on what's *behind* your request and show them how their commitment will be realized in the work you are doing. *(Hint: If you cannot find ways in which their commitments will be realized, it's doubtful you will get the help you want.)* There may be several commitments driving your action. If so, share all of them. As you do, speak for yourself and from your heart.

• *Step 3: Allow the people you are enrolling to involve themselves in the process.* It's a good idea to begin by giving them an opportunity to reflect and respond to what you have said so far. You might simply say, "How do you feel about what I've said?" Oftentimes, you will not have to say anything—stating your commitment will often elicit a response. Step three should be a rich conversation with plenty of questions and answers. You will be doing a lot of affirmative listening here. Oftentimes people will say, "So, what's the point?" or "Where's this going?"—giving you the perfect entrée to step four.

• *Step 4: Once you feel you have made your connection, move on to your request.* For example, "It's clear we both realize the importance of this task team, and what it means to our collective futures, and that's why I'm asking you to support the addition of another full-time team member beginning next week." You want your request to tie to the commitments you just discussed, but come right to the point and be clear. In that regard, this may be the shortest of the enrollment steps.

• *Step 5: Get a committed response.* You want a usable response—a yes or no, a counteroffer, or a promise to reply later. In essence, steps four and five form a *conversation for action.*

• *Step 6: Summarize the conversation and the outcomes.* As you summarize, be sure to emphasize again how granting your request will help them meet their commitment. Go on to thank the person or people involved.

You don't have to use these six steps per se. They are only a structure that ensures that, when making requests, you will lead with the commitment behind your request, rather than piling on reasons and benefits. Enrollment creates committed action. Committed action enables you to get all people can give, which is often more than you might request or expect. As you will discover in future chapters, commitment is a potent driver.

Like most important conversations, an enrollment should be planned. Here are some questions for each step to help you think through an enrollment process and plan the conversation.

For Step 1: Connect on a Personal Level

- What are one or two things the people I am enrolling are strongly committed to?
- What makes me say they are committed to these things?
- Do I share this commitment?
- What ways have I demonstrated my commitment?

For Step 2: Share Your Commitment

- What commitment is driving, or behind, my present effort?
- Is this commitment the same or similar to what the people I'm leading are committed to?
- What are the ways my successful efforts will satisfy both their commitments and my own?

For Step 3: Enrollment Conversation

- How do I expect people to respond to what has been said?
- How will I react, and what will I say, when they do respond?

- How would I like them to respond?
- What can I do to get this type of response?

For Step 4: Request

- Exactly what do I want, exactly when, and exactly whom do I want it from?
- What will happen or stop happening if I get what I want, and *when* will it start or stop happening?

For Step 5: Committed Response

- What are the four proper responses I will accept?

For Step 6: Summary and Closure

- Again, how will granting my request enable my commitments and theirs to be realized?

Enrollment works very well in most situations. However, there are circumstances where, even in the face of a strong common commitment and an exciting new possibility, you will be unable to enroll someone. This will be obvious before you get to step four in the enrollment process. You may notice and feel resistance, direct and indirect, to you and the possibility you are declaring. Oftentimes, this resistance won't seem logical. Using a prior example, when it's obvious that an individual has a big stake in the success of your task team, but that individual still won't help, something strange is going on. There is something preventing you from connecting and getting cooperation.

The majority of the time, when efforts to enroll someone fail, something out of the past has come up and intervened. As you are beginning to appreciate, mastering leadership conversation is an almost continuous struggle between the past and the future. And there is a distinction that will help you get a better grip on conversations and enable you to win this tug-of-war.

DEALING WITH "WATER UNDER THE BRIDGE"

There are few things in life we can accomplish alone. Most of the time we need the cooperation and help of other people. And one of the biggest barriers to getting that help and support is being *incomplete*.

As the term suggests, being incomplete refers to a process that is not finished—in this case, an internal process. A simple example of being incomplete would be if you receive a letter from a friend who is upset because you haven't responded to a prior letter. You may feel bad or be upset because cannot defend yourself and explain how chaotic your life has been in recent months. Whatever the reason, you will feel *the need to respond coupled with the inability to do so*. This mounting internal pressure you feel is incompleteness. Until you respond, this feeling will persist and probably grow in intensity. As long at it persists, this incompleteness will act as a barrier to your relationship. Let's say that before you can respond to that letter, your friend calls you up and asks you if you want to go to a party. Before you could respond, or maybe as part of your response, you would undoubtedly say something about why you never responded to the letter. You would get complete.

Notice that getting complete almost always involves a conversation. It *is* possible to reconcile an incompleteness internally. You can resolve it without discussing it with another person. However, even that might be considered a conversation you have with yourself. Regardless, the ability to hold conversations to complete the past is a critical leadership skill. No matter how appealing a new future might be, people can't go for it while part of them is stuck in the past. It's like swinging across monkey bars. People can have one hand reaching out in front, but they aren't going anywhere until they let go of the bar behind them.

LEARNING TO COMPLETE THE PAST

Getting someone to let go of the past is relatively easy. If you sense resistance to a new possibility or you are getting a half-hearted response, then you might initiate a conversation to complete the past. This is one of the few times, as a leader, that you will intentionally facilitate a conversation in the past domain.

Because each individual, group, and situation is so unique, there is no step-by-step process. Completing the past may have to do with complaints, unspoken opinions, misunderstandings, lies, hurt feelings, unexpressed appreciation or acknowledgment, any of a number of things. Because the reasons are diverse and usually unknown to you, it is nearly impossible for you to take the lead.

The key to completing the past is creating a context in which the reluctant or resisting person or group feels safe and able to finish a conversation that's been put on hold —maybe for years. The source of incompleteness may be personal or not. For example, if you intentionally or unknowingly hurt another person by something you did, the conversation will include you in a very personal way. On the other hand, if the source of incompleteness has to do with how a person feels about their poor performance on a previous assignment, it may have nothing to do with you. Either way, however, your role is to create an opening for them to speak and for you to listen. Completing the past is a conversation where you do little, if any, speaking.

If you are able to create a context and open the conversation, the rest will take care of itself. This is because pressure, stress, and tension build when people are left withholding an undelivered communication. If you create an acceptable outlet and a way to relieve the pressure and tension, people will usually take advantage of it.

Creating a context for completing the past will require that you put all your communication skills into play. It might include:

- Finding a private and quiet location.

- Expressing genuine concern—not just about the lack of action but about your relationship.

- Using extremely broad, general opening statements like, "What's going on?"

- Avoiding making judgments, or expressing any opinions or assessments. For example, don't say, "You obviously have some kind of problem, and I want to get at it."

- Listening with your heart as well as your head.

- Apologizing or forgiving only if it seems necessary and natural.

- And, as the conversation comes to a close, declaring completeness.

These last two points are important. There should be no expectation that a conversation for completing the past must include apologies or forgiveness. *The sole objective of completing the past is to deliver a previously unexpressed communication.* You need only listen and receive the communication. Anything else is icing on the cake.

The last thing you do is declare completeness. This serves two purposes. It tests to be sure that all parties involved are truly complete, and it ends this conversation and enables you to start a different one, or maybe finish an enrollment.

Holding a conversation for completing the past enables you to put others in action on a new possibility, and it also makes you aware of the whole notion of completeness and the power it has over you and others. With this awareness, you will be less likely to withhold a comment, thanks, complaint, or concern when you are having conversations. Even the smallest and seemingly insignificant message, if it is withheld, will have a negative impact on your relationships and your ability to create and maintain future-driven action.

Up to this point, the focus has been on the power of conversation that comes as a result of creating new distinctions for speaking and listening. In the case of completing the past, you are able to use conversation to gain access to an area that may have seemed inaccessible to you. However, what you will soon discover is that conversation is sometimes the only way to get into certain previously inaccessible domains.

9

CHANGING ORGANIZATIONAL CULTURE

___

Mastering conversation not only enables you to lead more effectively, it gives you access to areas that most people struggle to influence and change. In this chapter you will gain a better understanding of what culture is, how it shows up, and how you can change it.

Changing and shaping your organization's culture is every bit as important as creating and achieving a vision. Among other things, in a business organization, the culture drives the behaviors that shape the upper and lower limits of productivity. Moreover, because the culture dictates what's important, who's important, and what it takes to be successful, it has enormous impact on an organization's future direction. In short, it's impossible to substantially change the direction of your enterprise without changing the culture.

However, culture seems paradoxical. On some level you know what culture is. You talk about it, you feel its impact, and yet you and most other leaders struggle to put your hands on it. It's there, and yet it isn't. And there's a good reason why culture is so elusive.

LANGUAGE CREATES REALITY

It's possible to create distinctions for anything—even the universe itself. One of the most useful of these universal distinctions is to divide everything into two broad categories: things that exist in substance, and things that exist in language. For example, the book you are holding exists in substance. It has physicality. The knowledge you obtain from this book exists only in language. One is physically verifiable, the other is not.

Things that exist in substance are often measurable. You can usually use one or more of your five basic senses to experience them. You can't experience things that exist in language in the same direct fashion; you can only think and talk about them.

The reason this distinction is so powerful is that a great many of the problems human beings have are caused by confusing these two things. That is, we tend to treat things that exist in language as though they exist in substance. When we do, mischief occurs . . . and worse. The sixth principle you must apply to master the art of conversation is: *Distinguish between those things that exist in substance and those that exist in language, and act appropriately.*

Some of the things that exist in language include love, friendship, happiness, hatred, ambition, God, honesty. . . . These are the subject and focus of great stories. Wars are fought over these things. Most people will give almost all they have for *one* of these things that exist in language. In the end, it is the *intangible* things that are important in life. So it's natural that you pursue, obtain, and attempt to accumulate these things. And you tend to go about it as though you were pursuing physical objects, and this is where the difficulty begins.

Did you ever wonder about the many rituals that evolve around love—why saying "I love you" to someone for the first time is so stressful and significant? And, why it is that someone who says "I love you" wants to hear the same from you? It's because love exists and shows up for us primarily in the spoken word.

In a similar vein, why is it so difficult for some people to apologize? One of the oldest comedy bits features someone struggling to apologize—the words "I'm sorry" literally stuck in the throat. It's because forgiveness exists only in language.

At some intuitive level, you know that certain things only exist in language, and that realization shapes your behavior, but only to a degree. Maybe you hold onto a person you love, believing that if the individual is present their love will be also. Yet you can be sitting next to that person and wondering where the love went. Because you had love, you assumed it would remain, as a physical object would. To help you maintain that illusion, you may surround yourself with photos and tokens symbolizing wonderful times in your relationship, hoping to keep that happiness forever locked within those mementos. If so, you might be looking at those photographs through tears.

You probably struggle in many different ways to make the things that exist in language exist in substance. You often use symbols, tokens, and rituals to make the intangible tangible and accessible. That's one reason churches, temples, mosques, and other houses of workshop are so important to most people. These buildings and the rituals practiced inside are intended to help people to keep their faith. However, in the end, no symbol or ritual can make or keep a faith—or love, or anything else in that domain of existence. However, this is not to say that you cannot gain access to those things—shape, change, influence, and at times create those things. You can, and as a leader, you must.

Creating and attending to things that exist in language is the work of a leader because it is these things that motivate people and drive most human behavior. A leader needs followers. The things that exist in language are what attract and beckon to others—not only the future, but happiness, status, fulfillment, love, and the other internal qualities we value.

You can gain access to the things that exist in language through conversation. Sounds logical, and it is. Let's explore one of these—culture.

CULTURE: FRIEND OR FOE?

Your organization's culture can either be a powerful ally or a foe as you set your work group's or organization's future course.

Culture is the social environment of your business. Just as you need clean air, clear water, and decent food to live and prosper physically, you need a nurturing social environment to live with others. Your culture tells you how to be successful and how to view yourself and other people. It dictates your heroes, attitudes, and values. Your culture tells you what's important and who's important. It provides the unwritten rules you live by. Culture is probably the most powerful agent within a social system when it comes to shaping, influencing, and changing behavior. As such, it deserves a lot of attention from leaders.

Culture is difficult to change or influence for several reasons. For one thing, it affects and to a degree negates the behavior of those trying to change it. For example, if you were wanting to make your organization less paternalistic, you would have to go about it in a paternalistic manner, since other approaches would be rejected. In so doing, you would be acknowledging and reinforcing the behavior you are trying to change. Obviously this sends mixed messages. Despite this, there would seem to be little choice. If you act in a nonpaternalistic manner, cultural norms would not allow others to listen to you, let alone change. Changing culture seems to put people in a classic Catch-22 situation. You are damned if you do act in accordance with the culture when trying to change it, and damned if you don't.

An organization's culture is far more powerful than any individual. You don't have a culture, culture has you. For evidence of this you have but to look at the continuous criss-crossing of top-level executives from one company to another. One of the big advantages someone from another company offers is lack of indoctrination in the new organization's culture. However, the newcomer must act fast, because the acculturation process works with lightning speed, assimilating new people within a matter of days and weeks.

Another reason culture is difficult to change is that it seems inaccessible. If you have ever served as a member of a "culture team," you can appreciate this problem. Most individuals charged with shaping and changing a culture begin by *defining* it. After a time, any self-respecting culture team will then go on to describe the new or desired culture. This newly defined culture is then communicated to the rest of the organization, of course only after it is "blessed" by top management. Such efforts have limited impact, despite their general tendency to be on the right track.

Most culture change initiatives are more like glorified communications programs than business plans, and for good reason. *Culture is a conversation.* If this sounds strange, then listen up the next time you're hanging around the coffee pot, or eating lunch in the cafeteria. Listen to your culture.

Whenever I want to know the culture of an organization I'll be working in, all I have to do is go to three or four people and ask, "What's it like around here?" Or, "Tell me the way it is here." They will respond with cultural norms, values, beliefs, and rules for success—things like stay out of other people's sandboxes, learn to play golf, your clothes mean a lot, we really do care about people, and so on. These messages are repeated over and over again, passed from old members of the organization to new. The new members are quick to pick up on it, because speaking the culture makes them immediately acceptable. It's the "key to the club." Indeed, watch what happens if and when someone attempts to say anything that conflicts with the cultural conversation.

For example, if the general belief is that you need a college diploma to get ahead, observe what happens if you contradict that cultural statement. Even if you said, "A degree helps, but I think hard work is the key to advancement," heads will turn, snide comments will be whispered, and people may even take a few steps away. Countercultural conversation can create a gap between leaders wishing to change culture and their organization, if it is not handled properly.

CHANGING THE CULTURAL CONVERSATION

When people talk about culture change, what they really want is behavior change. Culture drives behavior, so the reasoning is, change the culture and you change behavior. This rationale is right, but it fails to take into account core beliefs—which are what drive culture. When someone speaks about changing the culture, what most people hear is "changing core beliefs," which is nearly impossible. However, it's not as hopeless as it sounds; you can reach into a culture and change it.

Because culture shows up as a conversation, you can shape culture through speaking and listening. The key, however, is speak about changing organizational behavior, *not* about changing the basic beliefs that underlie those behaviors. That is, when you speak about changing behavior, make a point of reaffirming the core beliefs or people will assume the underlying belief has also changed. When someone tries to introduce a new culture, it's tempting to focus on what is new and different. Unfortunately, that leaves people believing that *everything* is changing, or that the changes are bigger than they actually are. If people hold these assumptions, it is easy to see why most attempts to change culture meet resistance and often fail. Thus your message is subject to misinterpretation and rejection unless you acknowledge and preserve the underlying beliefs, and also address what is not changing as well as what you expect of the new behavior pattern.

In summary then, culture change conversations should:

- Point out those aspects of the existing culture that are not changing. Doing so creates credibility for you and keeps people from feeling that you are changing everything.

- Identify and clearly support the core belief or beliefs underlying the organizational behavior you wish to change.

- Show support and respect for the underlying belief by substituting another, more acceptable behavior consistent with that belief.

- Clearly state what behavior you wish to change or stop and why.

If you think of culture as a foundation of bricks, changing the cultural conversation is like carefully sliding out an old brick while simultaneously slipping in a new one—all the while leaving the "foundation" of core beliefs undisturbed. Many people make the mistake of saying things that make them appear to be pulling out one old brick after another. This leaves people feeling the walls are coming down. They are left staring at what appears to be gaping holes in their social foundation. Their attention is directed toward what is missing, rather than what still stands.

For example, let's say you're trying to change a tradition of developing people by promoting from within. Your new vision and direction requires that your organization quickly acquire new skills by hiring more people from the outside. This is a big cultural change. Here's one way to use this process and your knowledge about shifting conversations from the past to the present to make the change part of your corporate culture.

• *Step 1: Acknowledge the belief underlying the existing cultural norm, keeping it in the present and future to show that it is still important.* "We've always believed in developing people around here, and we still believe in that today."

• *Step 2: Openly acknowledge the existing practice or behavior that follows from that belief, clearly putting it in the past.* "In the past, we had a strong policy of promoting from within because it enabled our people to acquire new skills."

• *Step 3: Slip in a new practice or advocate a new behavior following from the basic belief.* "However, there are many ways to acquire new skills and to develop people. I am implementing a new program that will subsidize tuition for all employees at colleges, universities, and technical schools as a way to continue our commitment to development."

• *Step 4: Remove the old practice or behavior, clearly stating that the old behavior is no longer the norm.* "This tuition aid program is being implemented in part because we can no longer afford to develop people on the job. We need new skills faster than we can grow them with OJT, and sometimes we won't be able to wait for outside training, either. Our new direction requires that we begin to hire people with specialized new skills from the outside. We are no longer going to follow a strict policy of hiring from within."

To be sure, people will be shocked, angry, and upset at first. Managing a culture change conversation does not eliminate the normal and natural process that accompanies any significant change. However, most people will be able to work through the change curve if you have conducted a proper culture change conversation. The key is to focus on behaviors you wish to change, while at the same time acknowledging, preserving, and supporting the basic beliefs that underlie those behaviors. After all, it is the need to change organizational behavior that drives most culture change initiatives. Don't make the mistake of focusing on beliefs.

Of course, a good hard look at policies and practices is a natural part of any culture change initiative. They influence and shape behavior, and they must be consistent with the messages being communicated—which adds an additional step.

• *Step 5: Make sure you and the managers working for you do what you promised would be done.* In the current example, you would want to be sure that in filling positions, managers actively recruit people outside your organization in addition to posting the job internally—and that employees who come up with valid opportunities for training do get funding and time to take advantage of them.

Culture is only one of many elusive areas that you can access through the power of conversation. And, while the emphasis might seem to be on speaking, your effectiveness as a leader depends as much on how people listen to you as on how you speak. To a large degree, people's listening is shaped and influenced by how they perceive you. Therefore, developing and maintaining your image merits your concern and attention.

10

CHANGING YOUR IMAGE

How people perceive you—and how you perceive your-self—is critical to your success and happiness. The people you are leading react and respond, not really to *you*, but to their perception of you. As the saying goes, perception is reality. Likewise *your* behavior is shaped by your perception of yourself. Your self-image, which includes self-esteem, creates boundaries for how you think and act.

Creating a new future, the primary task of a leader, is risky and scary. You need a strong, positive self-image to take that risk. You need a solid, confident public image for others to follow and share that risk. Using the power of conversation, you can shape and project a powerful leadership image.

UNDERSTANDING WHAT MAKES IMAGE

When I say that perception is reality, I mean that you have to deal with a person's interpretations as though they were the truth. It doesn't mean you can't change that reality. You can change your personal and public image.

115

Because image is another one of those elusive things that exist in language, you can change your image by changing the conversation that creates and maintains it. This is particularly true of your external or public image. No one knows this better than public relations consultants and advertising professionals.

The entire PR and advertising profession is built on starting, broadening, and maintaining *conversations*— about people, products, places, and institutions. PR and advertising reaches out through radio, television, and print, billboards, talk shows, and books—all forms of public conversation.

PR and advertising is about creating and shaping image and perception. The objective is to make Jane and John Q. Public want a product, admire a person, visit a place, or put trust in an institution. And if you went to a reputable PR agency and asked them to improve people's perception of you, they could do it. However, such services are costly. Fortunately, you can use the very same approach, and many of the techniques used on Madison Avenue are within your reach.

Earlier I introduced you to *unspoken conversations*—the shared and silent conversations that shape perception and behavior. To sharpen that distinction further, think of image as an unspoken conversation. Image is a shared conversation—actually a story—that people tell about you and, at times, you tell about yourself. The use of the term *story* is appropriate because, as you can appreciate, your image is a mixture of fact and interpretation. At the very least, a person's image is generalized; it may well be a total fabrication. Usually it is a mix of the two.

Image is a generalization because it is likely that a good part of what others think and say about you is based on *one* incident, oftentimes an incident that only one person witnessed—the one who started the conversation. For example, if you really botched a presentation early in your career, there may well be a spoken and unspoken conversation about you that says that you are not a good communicator. Or maybe you have the one good oil painting you ever did hanging in your office, and as a result, there's a conversation circulating that you're artistic and creative. These conversational generalizations can work for you or against you. And they are relatively easy to shape and leverage because they have some basis in fact. However, that's not true of all aspects of your image.

There are parts of your personal image that are totally fabricated. These might result from an innocent but incorrect interpretation of something you do routinely, or they may be the work of a malicious colleague or competitor. For example, if you eat lunch in the quiet of your office every day, others might perceive you as a loner. This interpretation might become generalized over time and, before you know it, you see inexplicable comments in your annual appraisal—"not a team player." This seems unfair and ridiculous, and it gets worse.

Image can be created out of thin air. There are probably aspects of your image that have absolutely no foundation. Someone merely made up a story about you.

Have you ever sat in a doctor's office or stood on a street corner and watched a total stranger? When I do that, stories begin to spin in my head. Within seconds I have created a whole life for this stranger. This is a very common game, and players are mostly unaware of the catalysts—someone carrying a book may become an intellectual in the story, someone resembling a dear relative will pick up that relative's personality, someone seen through a haze of anger and irritation will turn into a jerk. None of these assumed characteristics has anything to do with the TV addict delivering the book, the ax murderer with the familiar face, or the saint who crossed the storyteller's path on a bad day—but they can be quite remarkably persuasive in the storyteller's mind, and long-lived as well, if the meeting turns into more than a passing encounter.

We all make up stories about other people all the time. These stories are based on the smallest bit of evidence, and oftentimes nothing at all. However, once fabricated, these internal conversations begin to look like the truth. And, when we share these stories with others, we tell them as though they are factual.

It may appear that we are talking about gossip. However, while people's perception is affected by gossip, your personal image is more. Gossip is often exaggerated and generally detracting. Image is both positive and negative, factual and fabricated. However, exploring the ways you deal with gossip can give you some insights into how you can shape and manage your own image.

GAINING ACCESS TO YOUR IMAGE

While not essential, it's helpful to have a picture of how others perceive you before you set about shaping and managing your personal image. However, you will never completely know how other people see you for two reasons:

• *The stories about you vary from person to person.* Your contacts and experiences with each individual vary, and everyone has different filters through which they view you. So even if someone comes clean and shares a complete and honest perception of you, you have only one set of perceptions, not everyone's.

• *People are reluctant to share that part of the story that might hurt, anger, or upset you.* Everyone's image of you is a mixture of positives and negatives, so there are aspects to the conversation about you that are like bad breath in the old ads. (Even your best friend won't tell you about it.) If you have a close friend or personal coach who tells you the whole story, you are blessed. Most people never have access to any version of the total story being told about them. Of course, you have bits and pieces, which is both helpful and not.

The part of your image that you have access to is generally the positive part people freely share with you. The part you don't have access to is generally the downside. Unfortunately, that's the part that causes problems for you on a daily basis.

Most of the time, you are left to piece together the less favorable aspects of your image based on your interpretations of how others act around you. For example, if you were to notice that you never get projects requiring a quick turnaround, you might suspect that people perceive you as slow. Or if you notice that each time someone wants to criticize something you've done, it takes forever to get to the point; you might begin to suspect that people see you as either overly sensitive or prone to anger. And there's the rub. Deciphering your personal image by interpreting the behavior of others is unreliable and usually creates more problems for you.

If you take action to change your image based on a *correct* interpretation of other people's behavior, you may tend to go about it in a defensive way—complaining, denying, or justifying. This usually has the opposite effect you want. Any defensive action related to shaping your image tends to reinforce the perception you wish to change.

If you take action based on an *incorrect* interpretation of what others think about you, it will confuse people and possibly create the very perception you are trying to change. After all, the thinking goes, if someone is denying or justifying, there may be something to it.

As with culture, the typical approaches to shaping and managing your image seem to put you in a no-win situation. If you don't address the negative aspects of your image, they will persist and cause you problems. If you attempt to take them on in a defensive manner, you reinforce them. It seems hopeless until you begin to think of image as pure conversation, and you begin to apply the basic distinctions you already have for speaking and listening. The seventh conversational principle is: *Consciously and intentionally manage and shape your own image as someone people listen to attentively.*

Creating Yourself in Conversation

The tendency for attempts to change your image based on the stories being told about you to backfire is another example of the endless cycle at work. However, as you know, you can break the endless cycle and create a new image and a new future by managing the conversation about you.

If you deny, defend, or justify a perception being held about you, you must give voice to that unspoken conversation, and this keeps it alive and circulating. For example, if I try to deal with a perception that I'm not a team player by saying "People say that I'm not a team player, but that simply isn't true," it won't change the story going around about me. And if I keep my mouth shut and go out of my way to demonstrate teamwork, people may interpret my behavior as an attempt to cover up or overcompensate. Even a genuine effort on may part will tend to lend credence to any negative perceptions. I'm in a no-win situation because I am speaking from the past and reinforcing a past conversation.

As with other conversations, speaking from the future means making declarations, in this case declarations about yourself. To create a new image, interject some new statements into the conversation going around about you. People are going to tell stories, so they may as well be stories that work for you. In this case, the term *stories* may not be so apt—the statements you make about yourself should have some basis in fact. If not, inconsistencies in your behavior will create a loss of credibility and you will lose your ability to manage and shape the perceptual conversation about you.

The notion of interjecting useful and positive statements about yourself may seem too simple to work, but it does. Indeed, you do it all the time. When you are introduced to others you will tend to distinguish yourself with short, often whimsical statements, things like "I'm the smart brother" or "I'm the pretty one." We also sprinkle descriptive phrases throughout our conversations, things like "I'm tough but fair" or "I'm not prone to exaggeration, so trust me." Despite how casual and unplanned such statements may seem, they significantly define and shape your image. If you begin to use this approach consciously and intentionally, you can manage and shape the perception others have of you. The key is to focus on aspects of your image that will make your job easier, while only *indirectly* addressing any negative perceptions others have of you. For example, if you wish to deal with a negative perception that you are not a team player, you might say that you value both individual initiative and team power. However, your overall efforts should be focused on creating something new, rather than addressing something from the past. There are some tricks you can borrow from the PR business.

Preparing and Planning Your Personal PR Campaign

There is a maxim in public relations called "the rule of threes." An effective campaign, the maxim holds, focuses on three primary messages and sends those messages via three communication channels within a three-month period. The objective is to break through the communications clutter and make an impact on the general public.

You can use the "rule of threes" in your own effort to shape and change your image.

• *Step 1: Identify the attributes that best describe your talents, shape the way people will perceive and listen to you, and enable you to accomplish your goals.* It's important to pick no more than two or three aspects to emphasize, because more than that tends to fragment and dilute the conversation.

It Takes Three to Tango

I had heard about the rule of threes, but never experienced its power until I consciously applied it in an effort to expand my coaching practice beyond business and professional people.

My credentials and experience—and consequently my image and reputation—as a personal coach to business executives were well established. The challenge was to change and expand my image to include people in all walks of life and of all ages. In particular, I wanted to work with families.

Employing the rule of threes, I concentrated on my local community. I wrote a series of short articles on coaching and offered them free of charge to editors of church, nonprofit, and governmental newsletters. Then I offered free seminars at local bookstores, church groups, and libraries. Finally, I sent copies of my last book along with a brief cover letter to local talk radio stations, offering my services as a guest interview. I made all three communication efforts in the same three-month period.

To be honest, while I got a response from each constituency, none of the communication efforts seemed to be an overwhelming success. I was becoming disillusioned and didn't hold any expectation that the rule of threes would work—but it did.

About four months after I began my personal PR campaign, I started getting phone calls from prospective clients. In the majority of cases, the people showing interest were unaware of my personal appearances and articles. In most cases, these people had not attended even one of my seminars, or heard me on the radio, or read one of my articles. Instead, they had heard *others* talking about me. In addition, most of the people who called me indicated that they heard my name come up more than once.

All of this unplanned research taught me two things about the rule of threes. First, that it works whether or not the communication event itself is successful, because it's not the statement or event that's important, but the conversation it starts. Second, it takes time to get results. The rule of threes works because image building and public relations is a conversation—and it takes time for the conversation to build.

Let's suppose you head up a product development function within a business organization, and you wish to develop and improve your image. You also want to create a context in which you can be creative and keep the political B.S. to a minimum.

Three positive statements that might serve you well in this situation would be: (1) You are a progressive, forward-thinking person. (2) You aren't afraid to take issue with top management. (3) You are creative and a little off-the-wall. Again, these attributes should be true; that's what makes them helpful. You want people to understand that you're the right person for the job because you are innovative and not stuck in the past. Also that you'd be effective in that position because of your ability to be a strong advocate for new products and for your function. And if people expect you to be a little wacky at times, you will have more options and greater freedom of action.

• *Step 2: Identify several communication channels through which you will send your three messages.* These channels can be conversations with different people, different events, different modes of communication, or all of these. In this case, it's okay to use more than three channels, but don't go overboard.

If you intend to send all your messages via people, try to pick people from three distinct areas of your life, or people with different relationships to the organization. Tell a colleague, your supervisor, an important customer, maybe a competitor. The idea is to disperse your messages as far and wide as you can, and if possible, to plant them with people who are in contact with many other people.

• *Step 3: Try to plant these messages in each of the chosen places three times within three months.* This is to ensure that the messages register and become firmly inserted into the network of conversation about you. It won't hurt to share these PR messages with others when the right opportunity presents itself. Over and over, and in different ways, interject your key messages—I'm progressive, I tell it like is, I'm creative and a little bit wacky at times. Of course, not all at once. Use tact, skill, and subtlety.

Then just sit back and wait. It may take several months before you get any confirmation that these messages are taking hold, but trust that a new, more powerful story is circulating. At some point, you will begin to hear other people repeating some or all of these messages back to you. You will be tempted to crack a smile when this happens, but don't. When a colleague says, "You're really a forward-thinking person," just say, "Thanks for the compliment." And don't be surprised if these messages show up in your next appraisal.

Managing and shaping your image via conversation seems too easy, too good to be true, but it works. It is particularly powerful when you are meeting someone for the first time. We all seem to have the need to put people in well-labeled boxes. That tendency is particularly pronounced when we meet someone new. So, when you're making a new acquaintance, be sure to insert your image-shaping messages into the introductory conversations.

CHANGE HOW YOU SEE YOURSELF

Conversation is the key not only to changing your public image, but also your private image—how you see yourself. Your self-image has more to do with what is possible in your life than your circumstances do. This maxim has proved itself in the lives of most great leaders from Catherine the Great of Russia to Martin Luther King Jr. Self-image creates the primary boundaries within which people think and act. Therefore it is an area that you need to explore and develop.

Self-image is the ground in which much of your behavior is rooted. Your perception of yourself determines your confidence, shapes your abilities, and dictates the degree of risk you're willing and able to handle. Self-image influences not only personal success but fulfillment. Success is getting what you want. Fulfillment is wanting what you get.

Even if you get what you go for, if you have a poor self-image, you may not feel a sense of accomplishment because you won't really believe that *you* made it happen. In short, *self-worth is the prerequisite for happiness.*

Happiness is obviously one of those elusive things that exist in language, and so are success and fulfillment. It should not be surprising then, that you can access, develop, and maintain self-image by managing conversation. In this case, conversations that take place mostly in your head.

Gaining Access to Self-Image

Self-image is a combination of how you think about yourself and how you think others feel about you. Together, these two sets of feelings create your personal picture of yourself. To change your self-image, you can focus on one or the other, since these aspects interact with each other. But let's start with how you feel about yourself, where those feelings begin, and how they developed.

As you might suspect, your parents created the initial version of your self-image. Beginning the moment you were born, the way they touched you, held you, and attended to your needs created the first feelings you had about yourself.

As you grew up and learned to talk, the way your parents talked to you, and in particular the way they described you, had an enormous impact on your self-image. Later on, what family members, friends, teachers, and others said about you built on that initial foundation laid by your parents. In short, self-image is the internalization of thousands of conversations about you. Once your basic perception of yourself was formed, probably by the age of five or six, it became a filter through which only those conversations that reinforced your perception could penetrate.

For example, if through countless conversations you came to believe that you are creative or dull, stubborn or weak-willed, handsome or ugly, you will tend to select and hear those parts of other people's conversation about you that fit that perception. On the other hand, you will tend to discount and invalidate any conversations that run contrary to how you see yourself. This is what makes changing self-image so difficult. Getting through the perceptual filters requires specialized conversations we typically associate with coaches, counselors, therapists, and others in the business of changing human mindsets. However, while you may decide to seek help from others, it's possible for you to improve your own self-image using the same techniques used by these professionals.

Improving Your Self-Esteem and Self-Image

There are countless books, tapes, and programs that focus solely on improving self-image and self-esteem. For the most part, they rely on a four-step process.
   • *Step 1: Get in touch with the negative conversations deeply embedded in your psyche.*
   • *Step 2: Loosen the grip of the negative perceptions you hold about yourself by exploring the possible sources of these self-destructive conversations and separate fact from interpretation.*
   • *Step 3: Develop new, powerful messages about yourself and systematically incorporate them into internal conversations about yourself.*
   • *Step 4: Watch for and deal with the recurring negative thoughts that come up as you repeat these new messages to yourself.*
The messages referred to in step three are called *affirmations.* An affirmation is a short, specific, positive, present-tense statement about yourself. For example, if past conversations—initially created by others and reinforced by self-talk—say that you are a dreamer, you might affirm, "I make my dreams come true."
   Dealing with the recurring negative conversation that comes up as you repeat your affirmations involves follow-

ing an internal conversation. If, when you say, "I make my dreams come true," your little voice responds with, "You're all talk," don't accept that. Think and say, "Not true. I act on most of my dreams." Continue this exchange until your little voice is quieter and weak enough to ignore.

The four-part process used to bolster and change how you see yourself is based upon the premise that because self-image was created by conversation, it can be penetrated and changed by conversation. It is a proven process, and one that's been around a long time because it works.

As noted earlier, changing self-image can start by focusing internally or externally. Wherever you begin, over time, how others perceive you and how you perceive yourself will become the same. That's not only a worthy goal, but a prerequisite to great leadership. Once again, the process of shifting conversations from the past to the present and future becomes the basic strategy for leadership development.

Initially, our discussion of managing conversations focused on *external* conversations. In the case of self-image, you must manage your *internal* conversations as well. When you do this, your life will fundamentally change. The biggest change will be the velocity at which positive changes occur in your life. Breaking out of the endless cycle, you'll leave incremental improvement behind, making quantum leaps and creating breakthroughs.

You already have most of the concepts, tools, and techniques needed to produce intentional breakthroughs. In the next chapter you will learn about the breakthrough process and how to apply what you have learned to accomplish extraordinary results.

11

CREATING
BREAKTHROUGHS
AT WILL

You have been managing and shifting conversations all your life. However, you've probably been doing it unconsciously and inconsistently. By creating distinctions for the ways you speak and listen, you become more effective and move more smoothly toward your goals and objectives. However, mastering the art of conversation not only enables you to achieve results more easily, it dramatically improves the kind of results you achieve. It gives you the ability to create intentional breakthroughs, and that's the focus of this chapter.

Breakthroughs are results beyond what you typically get or normally expect. If you look closely, you may find that you have experienced breakthroughs in your life. Learning a new language, attaining a degree in night school, or completing a difficult weight loss program qualifies. Breakthroughs come in all sizes and usually involve other people—oftentimes people we love. For example, when my 10-year-old daughter said she wanted to make movies,

I helped make that dream a reality. When members of a soccer team I coached came to me saying they wanted to win the championship, I helped put the trophy cup in their hands. You and I have many stories like this.

You may never have thought of these accomplishments as breakthroughs, but they fit the definition—results beyond what could normally be expected. And that's a good way to think of a leader. A leader is someone who consistently produces extraordinary results.

There are many people who are likable, lovable, and even inspirational. We call such people celebrities, icons, or stars, but you would only consider them *leaders* if they were catalytic in the accomplishment of some significant goal or objective. Therefore, the ability to create breakthroughs is the essential skill you should strive for.

ANATOMY OF A BREAKTHROUGH

If you have identified breakthroughs in your life, you know you have what it takes. Even if you haven't, you now have the distinctions to produce them at will. The ability to consciously and intentionally produce results beyond business-as-usual begins and ends with the conversations you create and foster. When it comes to producing breakthroughs, it's not a matter of whether you can or not—anyone can. The question is, exactly *how* do you do it?

Breakthroughs are few and far between, in part, because you don't know how you produce them. Not being able to put your finger on exactly what happened leads you to give away the credit for the accomplishment. You say, "I was just at the right place and the right time," or "It wasn't me, everything just came together like magic." When you give away the credit, you also give away your power to produce breakthroughs. After all, if you had little or nothing to do with producing a breakthrough, why would you think you could do it again? Understanding how you produce breakthroughs is the key to creating them whenever you wish.

If you take the breakthroughs you've identified in your own life and explore them, you will find that they have several things in common. Whenever breakthroughs occur, three things are always present: a new possibility, a strong commitment, and a lot of problems or breakdowns.

Whenever I share my insights on how breakthroughs are created, I often use popular movies like *Forrest Gump* to exemplify the breakthrough process at work. Take the Bubba Gump Shrimp Company as an example. As you may recall, Forrest Gump, a person with no experience in shrimping, below average intelligence, and no money, created a multimillion-dollar shrimping business. That's a breakthrough—and one of only many in this fictional character's life. Here's how the process worked.

• First the *possibility* developed. In this case, Forrest's good friend and army buddy Bubba, who knew something about shrimping, declared the possibility of going into business with Forrest when they finished their tour in Nam and went home. Notice this was a conversation. Forrest "signed up" for this without thinking. Ironically, Forrest had several advantages over most people. He was not smart enough to see possible difficulties, so he didn't second-guess himself and get sucked into past conversations. And his mother had helped him create a positive self-image.

• Next came the *commitment*, a deep heart and soul desire transcending logic and reason. For Forrest this commitment to go into the shrimping business sprang from his deep personal commitment to his friend Bubba, who got killed. This commitment initially grew as he and Bubba made plans—again, conversation. After Bubba died, Forrest declared his intention to go ahead with the plans he and Bubba had made. He had conversations with Lieutenant Dan, his mother, and others. His commitment grew.

• Once Forrest went into action, countless *barriers,*
problems, and *breakdowns* were encountered and overcome
before the final breakthrough result—the Bubba Gump
Shrimp Company—manifested. For Forrest Gump these
problems took the form of insufficient funds to get a good
boat and equipment, lack of skills, relentless competition,
and so on. Each breakdown, however, called up his commitment, and oftentimes evoked coaching, advice, and
help from others who shared his commitment—his
mother, Lieutenant Dan, and the rest.

Each of the three ingredients necessary to create breakthroughs involves conversation. Over and over again,
Forrest created a breakthrough in his work and personal
life by using conversation to create the breakthrough
ingredients. You can do the same if you have a clear, sharp
distinction for each of these three conversations.

MASTERING THE CONVERSATION
FOR POSSIBILITY

You already know how to create possibility when you speak
and listen. As discussed in Chapter 4, you use *declarations*
to shift conversations from the past to the future and
break an endless cycle. Declarations that begin with simple phrases like "What if—" create possibility. Once created, the possibility grows stronger and gathers supporters
as you continue to restate and reaffirm the possibility in
the face of contrary opinions.

Breakthroughs come in all shapes and sizes, and the size
of the breakthrough is determined by the gap between the
possibility and the current circumstances. The larger the
difference between the current circumstances and the
new possibility, the larger the breakthrough. Let's take an
example of market penetration for a particular product in
your business.

Let's say that your existing marketing and sales research reveals that you can expect to get a 3 percent to 5 percent improvement in market penetration this year. If you put out the possibility of 10 percent penetration, that would qualify as a breakthrough—it's double the best you might normally expect. However, if you said, "I think we can increase market penetration by 30 percent this year," that would be an even bigger breakthrough.

The bigger the gap between the new possibility and the current circumstances, the bigger the potential breakthrough. Figure 11-1 sketches the way this works. The key for leaders, of course, is to know how big a gap a person, group, or organization is capable of successfully taking on.

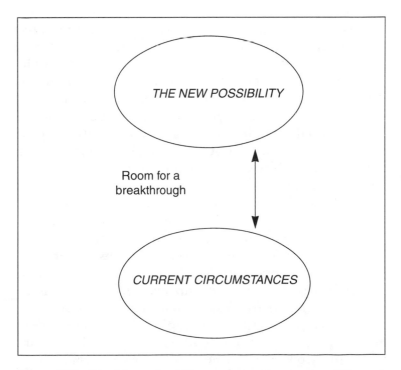

Figure 11-1 The bigger the difference between a new possibility and the way things are now, the bigger the breakthrough you can achieve.

This is not to say that a possibility should *seem* doable. Indeed, a good possibility usually seems impossible at first. Where you set the mark is determined by the ability of the team, the quality of relationships, the degree to which each player has a stake in the results, and other factors.

It would be good to point out, before we go further, that breakthroughs aren't always quantitative and about achieving more. Breakthroughs can occur with respect to time, and in qualitative areas of your life. For example, it might normally take 20 days to produce and implement a marketing plan, but you and your team decide to do it in 3 days. Or you might go for a breakthrough in the quality of your relationship with a coworker or a spouse. Regardless of the form a breakthrough takes, the process always begins with a declaration and a conversation that engenders understanding and support, one that successfully withstands initial efforts to invalidate it with opinions, assessments, criticism, and skepticism coming from others.

Oftentimes, the breakthrough objective is identified in the course of managing what can be called a *conversation for possibility*. Using our previous example, you might declare that a 30 percent increase in market penetration is a worthy goal. And, in the course of conversational give and take, your team might settle on 20 percent. Since it is well beyond the expected 3 percent to 5 percent, this would still qualify as a significant breakthrough.

You might feel strongly about achieving 30 percent. Maybe you have a genuine business need to reach a 30 percent target—but until you and the people you work with have a few intentional breakthroughs under your belt, it is more important that you break out of the mode of producing incremental improvements than it is to achieve an enormous breakthrough right off the bat.

Initial success is critical to keeping yourself and others in a breakthrough mode. With each succeeding breakthrough effort you will be able to create greater and greater achievements, stretching the gap between current circumstances and new possibilities. Success will also make it easier for you to generate and maintain commitment to the goal or objective, which goes hand in hand with the creation of possibility.

TAPPING THE POWER OF COMMITMENT

Commitment is another of those things that exist in language, so you have access to it by the way you speak and listen. Commitment has a big impact on results—greater achievements are possible when more commitment is present. You might think of commitment as a kind of energy that gives your actions their power. The more commitment there is behind an action, the more potent and effective it is. You can find evidence of this in your own life.

One of the best places to look for evidence of the power of commitment is to reflect on your relationship with those you love. Since love and commitment go hand in hand, action you take to help those you love is usually *committed action.*

Imagine that you meet a stranger on a bus who is depressed because he just lost his job. You might console him, offer advice, and even give him a few names and numbers to call. However, your actions would be quite different if your spouse, son, or daughter came to you with the same problem. You would not only offer emotional support and coaching, you'd call your friends and contacts in an effort to line up job interviews, you'd sit down to work on a new résumé, and you might even discuss the possibility of quitting your job and going into business together. In short, committed action is more powerful and effective.

You won't achieve breakthrough results without committed action. Therefore, as a leader, you will want to be able to create and maintain commitment.

GENERATING AND MAINTAINING COMMITMENT

Although the two are not the same, there is a positive correlation between the level of commitment you are able to generate and the stake you have in the achievement of a particular result. For instance, there are many good reasons for simplifying our lives. A simpler life is less stressful, more exciting, and oftentimes more fun. Any and all of these reasons might generate a commitment on our part to make significant changes in our lifestyles. However, if you or I were in ill health and our doctor suggested that our survival depended on being able to dramatically slow down; then we would be so committed to changing our lifestyle that *nothing* would stand in our way. Putting our survival at stake would definitely generate powerful action. And herein lies one way to generate commitment.

Commitment can be generated by identifying what is at stake for you and others in going for a breakthrough—or by putting something at stake for yourself and others. "At-stakeness" would seem to exist or not, but the truth is, you can create it. You do it all the time.

Say you are interviewing for a new job. You realize that this position might be made to order for you—a good skills match, an exciting new project to work on, and a welcome increase in income potential. These thoughts and internal conversations generate enough commitment for you to go to your supervisor and request that she support your candidacy. She does.

As you prepare for the interview, you have a conversation with your supervisor in which she points out that getting this position will put your career back on track. She also mentions that it would justify her confidence in you and reflect well on the whole department. Suddenly the added significance of this job interview begins to set in. You have more riding on it than you first realized.

Then you go home to discuss the possibility with your family. Your spouse is proud, happy, and excited. You and your family talk about the ways the extra money might be used. Suddenly you realize a lot is at stake in the upcoming interview—your career, your image in the eyes of your colleagues and your family, your ability to provide for your loved ones. You are more committed than ever to getting this new job, and your actions reflect it. This commitment was generated in conversations with your supervisor and family members.

Conducting a conversation in which you identify what is at stake, or finding things you can put at stake, is one way to do this. And there are other ways as well. If you want to experiment with generating and maintaining commitment, try the following:

1. Think of some action you are committed to taking. Maybe you want to lose weight, or stay more in touch with a family member, or stop smoking, or take up a new hobby—whatever you really want, and haven't managed to start.

2. Next, write down what you intend to do.

3. After a while, tell a family member or friend what you plan to do. In addition, say they can share this information with others if they wish.

4. Finally, as time goes on, observe what happens when you hear someone else talk about your intentions and plans.

The learning in this little exercise comes from noticing how you feel and what actions you take after each of the four steps. Each step is designed to generate more and more commitment.

The first conversation is a private, internal conversation. If you stopped here, the odds are nothing much would happen. We continually think about things we intend to do, but few of these thoughts ever become reality.

The second conversation is a written one. It is still private, but writing it down makes it more tangible. It is more than a thought, and it's in a form that could easily be shared with other people.

The third conversation is a turning point. Sharing an intended action with another person immediately increases the odds that you will act.

Finally, when your intentions begin to be shared with more and more people, you might feel that you have little choice but to take action. You'll probably go on a diet, call and write your family member regularly, join a smoking cessation program, or do whatever it is you said you would do. As your declaration includes more and more people, greater and greater commitment is generated, along with the odds for powerful action and success.

A simple example of this phenomenon at work can be seen when a management team develops a vision. Prior to the initial meeting, the conversation is a private thought process about what is possible. Then comes the meeting and the creation of the vision statement—all the participants in their speech and actions demonstrate and state their personal commitment to achieving the vision. Then they share the vision with others. As pointed out earlier, the transition from private to public conversation marks a significant turning point. A high level of commitment develops, often symbolized by personal appearances by members of the executive team, along with elaborate meetings. And even more commitment develops when the vision finds its way into the national press. There's no turning back now.

The visioning process is a growing conversation designed to increase commitment and assure that a dramatic change in direction takes place. Indeed, by the time the employees learn about the vision there seems to be little chance of backing out. The conversation, which began as a private one among a small group of people, suddenly grows beyond them. This loss of control accounts for the "my God what have I done" feeling that often strikes executive teams as they prepare to communicate their new vision.

You can use the same process to generate commitment to a breakthrough goal. As you are discussing the new possibility, encourage everyone to speak. Listen for public declarations of support. When someone declares support or promises to take action, make sure they know you and others heard them. Go around the table and ask each person to speak. Request that team members hold conversations with others about the breakthrough objective, go public with your plan in the company paper. In short, manage the conversation by enlarging it to include as many people as possible. Most important, find ways for each person to go public with declarations of support. Make sure everyone makes the transition from a private, internal conversation to a public one. Don't assume silence means support. Indeed, in a conversation designed to generate commitment, silence often indicates subconscious or even overt opposition.

It is not uncommon for people who are engaged in a conversation for possibility to want more time to consider a response. It may be necessary to allow this, but you are taking a risk if you do. Left to think things over, most of us will inevitably get caught up in the drift to the past, and future possibilities tend to disappear. If you are unable to get a verbal commitment in the moment, be sure to follow up with one-to-one coaching and conversation that identifies and creates "at-stakeness."

Oftentimes, when someone is unable or reluctant to commit to a breakthrough, it is because they are already imagining and anticipating the problems that will inevitably follow. If so, you may have to deal with these imagined problems before you can get the commitment you want and need.

THERE ARE NO PROBLEMS

Problems are another of those pesky things that exist in language. What we call a problem is simply an event or circumstance with a negative interpretation attached. This notion is not some Pollyanna philosophy of positive thinking. Problems do not exist in substance.

The intellectual understanding that our interpretations of events create problems does not help us deal with our own and other people's reactions when something stops us and interferes with our plans. When this happens, we can't help but feel that something is wrong. And it is this thinking that keeps us from achieving more breakthroughs in our lives.

If your reaction to problems is "something is wrong," you usually reassess the situation. This alone creates delays and slows down activity. However, problems trigger a whole range of behaviors that make life more difficult.

Oftentimes, as a result of a reassessment, you will take different actions. If the problems appear too big, you may compromise your goal or give up altogether. Maintaining flexibility and creativity is important, but when problems occur, you can end up generating more activity than is necessary; you waste time and energy, compromise your objectives, and oftentimes damage working relationships. This deterioration in relationships occurs as a result of the blaming that inevitably ensues when problems surface.

Blaming is an attempt to put distance between yourself and problems. You feel the need to create this psychological distance because you think of problems as something that *should not be happening*. Since, distinctions change how you see things, when you distinguish problems as an indicator that something is wrong, you behave accordingly. Therefore, it might be helpful to redistinguish problems. Indeed, it is critical that you begin to see problems in a new way if you want to create breakthroughs.

How Much Is Enough?

If you are a parent, you can look forward to, or recall, the time when college education for a son or daughter looms on the horizon. As that fateful day approached for my daughter, my wife and I found ourselves lamenting our personal financial situation. We had a problem. We didn't have enough money to provide the kind of education we wanted for our daughter. However, the prospect of financial aid gave us new hope.

We made inquiries, gathered information and forms, and went about the tedious and humbling process of filling out several financial aid applications. There before us in black and white was a list of all our worldly assets—bank accounts, cars, home equity, stock portfolios, income tax returns, and statements of "expected earnings." While the application process was disappointing and humiliating in some ways, my wife and I realized that our lack of means was now an asset. The less we had, the more qualified we were for financial aid. Our lack of funds was no longer a problem . . . but not for long.

Some time after submitting our applications we received a letter stating that we had too much money to qualify for financial aid. Once again we had a problem, only now the problem was that we made too much money.

Our income and assets never changed during the 3-month period during which we sought to finance our daughter's higher education. However, we initially had a problem because we didn't make enough money. Then not making enough money was beneficial and no longer a problem. But in the end we had another, totally unexpected problem: we discovered we were making too much money. How can this be?

It happened because problems are relative. They don't exist as substance, but only in language. That's particularly true of money problems. How much is enough? Ask five different people and get five different answers.

GAINING A NEW PERSPECTIVE ON PROBLEMS

Problems always seem unwelcome, and they can be the enemy of anyone wishing to create extraordinary results. Problems stop action and trigger assessments, evaluations, judgments, and opinions. This behavior shifts the drift of conversation into the past. Action driven from those assessments creates incremental improvement as opposed to a breakthrough. This shift in conversation and action often shows up as a compromise. When you make a compromise, it may appear you are not loosing much, but you are usually giving up the possibility of a breakthrough.

Think for a moment about the term *breakthrough*. What you are *breaking through* is the past. By definition, a breakthrough is a break with the past, a change in the status quo.

Any change creates resistance that shows up as problems. Problems are the predictable and natural resistance you encounter any time you attempt to take action on a new possibility. The bigger the change, the bigger the problem—or the more problems there are. So when you are attempting to make huge changes or breakthroughs, you can and should expect problems to arise. Indeed, problems are an indicator that you're making a significant change. Problems should be happening, particularly when you are creating breakthroughs—if things seem to be going very smoothly, you probably aren't making as much progress as you think.

Distinguishing problems as something that *should be happening* does not totally put an end to the emotional turmoil you experience when they arise, but it does enable you to catch yourself and others being caught up in the conversational drift toward reassessment, reevaluation, judgments, opinions, and the rest.

Holding this new distinction for problems—as something that should be happening—diminishes the negative impact they have on your behavior. Indeed, problems can be affirming and ultimately even comforting. After all, when problems show up, it means "something is right." You are making change and possibly headed for a breakthrough.

Of course, you do still have to address problems. But having a more empowering distinction for problems enables you to do so without compromising your objectives or goal. If you and those you are working with can maintain your commitment to your original breakthrough goal, you will be successful.

THE BREAKTHROUGH PROCESS

Managing internal and external conversations is the key to intentionally creating results beyond business-as-usual. The differences between the normal decision-making and problem-solving process and the breakthrough process may seem small, but they are fundamental.

With the traditional management process illustrated in Figure 11-2, an issue, concern or problem is presented; people offer opinions, assessments, and interpretations

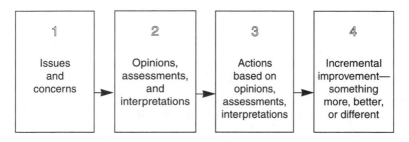

Figure 11-2 The traditional management process, in which action is based on past-domain conversations, produces incremental improvements.

about what's causing the problem and how to solve it. Eventually, generally after a near-endless round of opinions and other conversation from the past, people begin to align around a particular cause and solution. Action is taken based on a consensus of opinions, and it's pretty well bound to be cautious and limited action—another slow turn of the endless cycle.

As with any action based on past-domain conversation, incremental improvement will result because the process entails taking what already exists and making it more, better, or different. While this traditional management process yields results, it does not create fundamental change, quantum leaps, or breakthroughs.

The eighth and last principle you must apply in order to master leadership conversation is: *Go for a breakthrough.*

The breakthrough process illustrated in Figure 11-3 begins with declaration and new possibilities. Rather than a proposal to change what already exists, something totally new is on the table. People act on those possibilities that offer the best chance of creating a breakthrough. This is different from choosing the path of least resistance and going with actions that will be relatively easy to implement. Indeed, the possibilities that will make the most problems will oftentimes create the biggest breakthrough.

These conversations for possibility and opportunity, as well as the requests and promises that generate action, are all conducted in a manner that generates commitment. This means that all those involved identify what's at stake for them and publicly declare their support, and that someone is there to initiate coaching conversations when people ask for them or seem to need them. If this happens, alignment and action based upon a future possibility will almost always deliver a result beyond business-as-usual.

Such future-driven action inevitably creates resistance and problems or breakdowns. However, this time, problems are *expected* and even *wanted* because they are an indication that fundamental change is taking place.

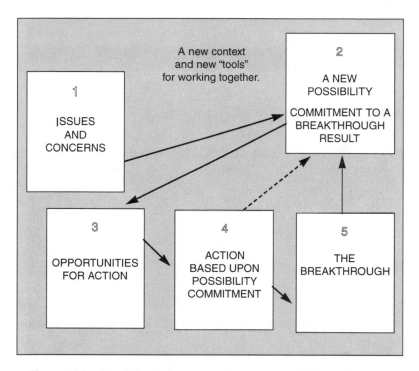

Figure 11-3   Breakthroughs come when new possibilities drive committed action.

That's the breakthrough process. Now you have everything you need to create intentional breakthroughs—the distinctions, the skills, and the know-how to put them all together. Creating breakthroughs is harder than making incremental improvement, but it's one of the skills that distinguish truly great leaders.

Only one question remains: Where should you start? To find out, ask yourself, *"What is impossible to do today, but if it were possible, would totally transform my business?"* Answer that, and you're on your on your way to a challenging and exciting new future.

12

MANAGING BUSINESS AND PROFESSIONAL CONVERSATIONS

By now you realize that the term *mastering*, as applied to conversation, is not the same as *controlling*. And that will become even clearer as you apply the distinctions and use the processes and techniques you've acquired throughout your workday.

The previous chapters have given you the distinctions, speech acts, and techniques needed to master the art of conversation. This chapter will refine those distinctions and help you develop the finesse you'll need in business and professional situations. Leadership is a subtle art. You must learn to apply the principles outlined in this book with precision, consistency, care, and ingenuity. The step-by-step process at the end of this chapter will bring everything together.

In most situations, the larger the number of people participating in the conversation, the more powerful it is. For instance, the conversation about "the way it is here," the culture conversation, is extremely powerful because it includes nearly everybody associated with a group or organization, even those not directly affiliated with it. But culture is only one of the conversations that have a significant impact on people's behavior at work.

All unspoken conversations, like those that create your public image, are strong because they include everyone you have ever been in contact with, as well as people who have only heard about you. Your image creates the boundaries you operate within and has an enormous impact on your life. Such conversations are, at times, more powerful than you are.

Recognizing and respecting the innate power of large, shared conversations is an important component of mastery. For if you attempt to exert the verbal equivalent of brute force to *control* conversations, odds are you'll come up the loser.

Mastery has more to do with *guidance* than control. When you participate in a conversation, it is possible to guide and direct the flow of the conversation by periodically interjecting statements that ultimately deflect the course of the conversation and make it go in the general direction you want. Mastering the art of leadership conversation is more like aikido than boxing.

As you may know, aikido is a primarily defensive Japanese martial art. *Aikido* translates as "the loving way" because it enables you to protect yourself without harming another—and that's what conversational mastery is about. Getting what you want without hurting others.

Unlike boxing, where you stand toe to toe with an opponent and slug it out, blocking punches and jabbing at each other, in aikido you use subtle movements to avoid blows, giving you the opportunity to turn your opponent's attacks back on themselves.

If you have ever boxed or been in a real fight you know that blocking a punch hurts almost as much as being punched. But if you watch carefully when an aikido master faces that same sort of punch, you will see the master move slightly to one side or the other, or use an open hand or a couple of fingers to slightly deflect the blow so it misses. It may only miss by an inch, but that inch means the difference between being hit and being safe. Such should be the process when you manage conversations.

MANAGING THE FLOW OF A CONVERSATION

Conversations will contain a large proportion of opinions, assessments, and interpretations—past-domain statements. You will continually be struggling to guide the conversation into the future and the present by interjecting declarations, requests, and promises. As you do so, it will feel like you are swimming upstream against the conversational flow. And that is true until others begin to engage and contribute to the conversation for possibility and action you start. As more people begin to participate, your conversation will gain power. Eventually the conversational flow will change course and you will have successfully shifted the conversation.

You don't need to have even half of the people participating join in a present- or future-domain conversation to make the shift. That's because conversations for possibility and action are driven by a strong commitment that makes them more compelling, exciting, and powerful. The proportion of people engaged in shifting a conversation will vary from circumstance to circumstance. However, when the shift occurs, it will be relatively dramatic and obvious, especially to you. Anyone who has been involved in a difficult negotiation knows what this is like.

A troublesome negotiation is a quagmire of conversation from the past—accusations, charges, opinions, judgments, stories, name calling, the whole litany of frustration. It is a conversation, in grisly detail, about things that happened yesterday. If the negotiation is to be successful, one or more participants will have to break this endless cycle and declare some new possibilities. For example, if the issue being negotiated has to do with lay-offs necessitated by the need to cut expenses, a conversation for possibility might begin with, "I think we can find a way to give you job security, if you can help us find another way to keep costs down."

Such statements will initially fall on deaf ears. It will take countless declarations like this on your part before you hear these possibilities echoed back. When this happens, it is a sign that your conversation is growing to include others.

Often, shortly after the sign that your conversation is being shared, a dramatic shift occurs. This is the sudden breakthrough you often experience in a difficult negotiation process. If the total negotiation process takes ten days, nine and a half days will be spent in mostly useless reiterations of the past. It might only be in the last four hours that the negotiators begin making progress—and literally at the last minute when the negotiations suddenly reach a successful conclusion.

When the conversational shift occurs, it oftentimes happens quickly and dramatically. You and others will sense new energy and excitement. And you are often left wondering why it took so long to get to this point. What you will come to realize is that, because most conversation is driven from the past, a certain amount of time will be spent and wasted speaking and listening in a way that makes no difference. However, as your skill and ability in managing conversation improves, you'll find yourself in groups that waste less and less time. And as you become more comfortable using the concepts, skills, and techniques in this book, you can cut the amount of wasted time dramatically. Take something as simple as phone calls.

In my own observation of my clients at work, I discovered that the average business phone call lasts 12 minutes. When my clients applied the principles involved in mastering the art of conversation, they were able to reduce their average phone call to 7 minutes. That's a 40 percent savings. If you have 12 phone calls a day, you gain a whole hour of additional time. And, you can save even more time if you apply these principles to meetings and other conversations.

Planning Conversations

Planning is an essential business and professional skill. You do marketing plans, budget plans, ad campaign plans, career plans, and so on and on. However, planning conversations will enable you to do everything else, including business planning, faster and better.

No doubt you plan meetings and create agendas, but planning conversations is different. You don't need to plan *every* conversation you have, but rather the ones that will have a major impact on your career and your organization's future. Before you begin any significant conversation, it is always beneficial to:

- Do a "listening inventory."
- Generate a clear commitment of your own.
- Identify *specifically* what you expect and want to happen as a consequence of the conversation.

The term *listening inventory* refers to an introspective process where you get in touch with the way you tend to listen to the other people who will be involved in the conversation, and how these same people may perceive and listen to you. The purpose of this preparatory step is to enable you to manage your reactive listening and disempower any "negative listening" others might have for you. Chapter 7 explored both these areas, but it may be useful to sharpen the distinctions now.

Disarming Background Listening

The notion that each of us operates amid unspoken conversations is useful whether you apply it to yourself or others. There are stories and labels attached to you and everyone you know. As with most stories, they are a mixture of fact and fantasy. Some of the things people say about you are true, other things are not. The same is true for what you say about other people.

As pointed out earlier, these widely shared stories about people become a kind of filter for incoming information. Like any filter, this one lets certain things in and keeps other things out. Even if the unspoken conversation is generally positive and good, it is always limiting because it still filters information out. Suppose people say, for example, that you're a genius. That's good. However, if it keeps people from questioning your judgment so they let a plan or recommendation of yours move ahead with fatal flaws, that's bad. (Likewise, if you catch yourself thinking, "He must know what he's doing," stop. The implications you were about to dismiss may be enough to derail the whole idea if not they're dealt with now.)

Most of the time, unspoken conversations are a mixture of positive and negative stories. The negative ones definitely affect the way you listen, and ultimately the direction and outcome of the conversation. It is possible and relatively easy to get in touch with the way you listen to others. Just think about what you and others say about a particular person. And, while it is not as easy, you can get in touch with what other people say about you, and consequently with the way they listen to you.

This background listening, whether it is attached to you or others, exists separate from any perceptions developed during the conversation. It *precedes* the conversation and is already in place and in play *before* the conversation begins. Being aware of your background listening enables you to do two things:

First, with regard to other people, getting in touch with your background listening better enables you to catch yourself listening that way, and begin listening affirmatively—listening for possibility, commitment, partnership, and other useful things.

Second, getting in touch with the background listening others have about you prepares you to disempower it by speaking about it without acknowledging it. For instance, if the mostly unspoken conversation about me says that I like to work alone, somewhere near the start of the conversation, I might say, "I sometimes like to work alone, but I'm excited about the opportunity to work hand in hand with all of you on this project." Such a statement, especially if it is repeated in different ways, and at different times, will help keep people from incorrectly interpreting some statement or action on my part as supporting their mostly erroneous perception of me.

For example, another person, who doesn't have a "not a team player" image, would be able to offer to lead a project and people would see it as a demonstration of commitment and leadership. If I—with my image as a loner—did the very same thing, people might be prone to see my offer as an attempt to take control and minimize the need to work with others. The same action elicited two different interpretations created by two different kinds of background listening. More important, it evoked two different reactions and probable outcomes.

Doing a listening inventory is important because it ultimately affects reactions, results, and outcomes. Everything we create begins with a conversation, and every conversation is shaped by the way you and others listen. So, contrary to how it might appear, the most powerful part of conversation is listening, not speaking.

Following the listening inventory, there are two more preparatory steps—generating personal commitment and developing a clear and specific idea of what you want to happen as a consequence of the conversation.

GENERATING PERSONAL COMMITMENT

All committed action, including committed speaking, is extremely powerful and should serve as the foundation from which you operate. Generating commitment results from getting in touch with what is at stake for you in this conversation, and oftentimes, putting additional things at stake. Again, this concept was introduced earlier (in Chapter 8) but not put in the context of a business or professional conversation.

The process of generating commitment involves tracing the source of your actions to their root cause. For example, say you're about to have a meeting to determine how much of next year's training budget you can cut. This will not be a fun meeting. How you approach this conversation, and particularly how you speak and listen, will reflect the clarity and depth of commitment you and others feel.

If you didn't think about it, the commitment driving your behavior might be superficial. For many people, it would be a commitment to hold on to as much of the current budget as possible. Such a commitment will set you and others up for a confrontational meeting. You may feel strongly about keeping your section of the budget intact, but such a self-centered commitment will not generate the personal power you want and need. Moreover, it will not touch those whose listening, understanding, and cooperation you will probably need. Dig deeper.

You might get in touch with your personal commitment to help and develop people. You might realize that you also hold a commitment to the future success of the company that has been pretty good to you over the years. And, if you go deeper still, you might also realize how your job has made it possible for you to give not only food and shelter, but education and a great lifestyle to your family and those you love. If you approach this hypothetical budget meeting and speak from, and oftentimes of, your commitment to help others, your commitment to the long-term success of the company, and your gratitude for past blessings, you will speak and act totally differently than you would if you went in fighting tooth and nail for your budget.

Even if you wish to keep as much of your budget as possible, the realization that you are also committed to developing other people and to the long-term success of the organization will show up in your words and actions and make it easier to deal with others in this matter, because they share these commitments. More important, in trying to reconcile what seem like diametrically opposed commitments—cutting training to reduce company expenses and continuing to promote the development of your people—you may be a catalyst for creating some new possibilities for doing both. What starts as a budget-cutting meeting could end up creating a breakthrough.

If it's not your style to talk about what's at stake for you and what you are committed to, just holding it inside you will have a beneficial effect. More important, you will be setting and keeping yourself on a course that will enable you to get what you really want in life. This last point is worth contemplating.

GETTING WHAT YOU REALLY WANT

There are probably times in your life when you look around and wonder how you got where you are. Maybe you find yourself in a job you hate, or a relationship that doesn't give you joy, or a place far away from those you love and care about.

If you are lucky, you may be able to trace your journey to certain events and specific conversations that ultimately led to your present circumstances. And if you look deeper, you may find that, during those turning-point conversations, you were not in touch with, or acting in accord with, your deepest commitments. You were out of touch with what was really important to you.

If there is a key to happiness and success, it would have to be acting in harmony with your deepest commitments.

You won't always come out on top, but in the long run you will get more of what you want most of the time.

Committed speaking and listening drives powerful action. And having a clear idea of the actions and outcomes you want from any given conversation is a critical part of preparing for all conversations, particularly those in a business and professional setting.

Determining Outcomes and Conditions of Satisfaction

There are times where you want to go into a conversation with no agenda other than to have fun or learn. However, with many conversations it's important to identify and communicate desired outcomes and your specific conditions of satisfaction at the outset. Having your needs and expectations clearly delineated *before* your conversations will greatly increase your chances of getting what you want.

Outcomes might include agreements, understandings, actions, promised actions, or maybe just a new or improved relationship. Conditions of satisfaction include the circumstances and context within which you achieve your outcome. For example, agreement to cut the budget at least 10 percent is an outcome. Doing it without reducing full-time staff or missing production targets are conditions of satisfaction. The key here is being specific.

When you are planning an important meeting with other people, identifying desired outcomes and conditions of satisfaction seems to be a normal and natural process. However, when you're not collaborating with others, this step sometimes gets glossed over or lost. By knowing specifically what you want and under what conditions, you will be able to:

• Formulate clear requests and promises from the start.

- Immediately negotiate counteroffers and avoid additional meetings.
- Reduce misunderstandings and mistakes.
- Shorten the overall length of most conversations and meetings.

Identifying desired outcomes and conditions of satisfaction is normally an unconscious process. When it is, you sometimes need two or three conversations to accomplish what you could have in one. And worse, you occasionally find yourself taking action or agreeing to action that you later regret.

Take something as simple as trying to get some feedback from your boss on your performance. You want and need some quality face-to-face time and a context that will facilitate open, honest feedback. You decide that a lunch meeting would do the trick. You call to invite the boss, asking if she is available for lunch tomorrow. She accepts. All seems to be going well until the boss shows up with a new customer who's visiting. She says, "I wanted you to meet our newest client, so this lunch worked out perfect." Perfect indeed. This frustrating situation occurred because you did not clearly formulate and communicate your desired outcomes and conditions of satisfaction.

Once you complete your listening inventory, generate a clear commitment, and identify desired outcomes and specific conditions of satisfaction, you're finally ready for the actual conversation.

Getting the Most Out of Business Conversations

You already have a useful distinction for managing conversations. In general, it is a process whereby you guide the natural flow of the conversation away from the past. Your guidance begins with listening and being aware of which realm of time the conversation currently occupies, and

Satisfaction

You may recall the story about one of my coaching clients who called and begged me to come to a meeting, when what he wanted was for me to stop a couple of task team members who were constantly bickering, wasting time, and dividing the team into warring camps. Here's some more of that story.

My client finally got around to making a proper request and now needed to come to terms with his conditions of satisfaction. I could have asked him directly, but I wanted to make a memorable point. So I asked, "Why don't you just remove one of the troublemakers?"

"No, no. I need both of these people on the team," my client responded. "They are subject matter experts, and figure in politically as well."

"Okay," I came back, "Which one do you think is causing the problems? I think I can take him down a peg or two."

"I don't want that," the team leader said with obvious concern. "I think they both contribute to the problem . . . and I don't want either one of them to think I was bitching about them behind their back . . . then I'll get mixed up in their infighting."

I had discovered three conditions of satisfaction so far. One was that my client wanted to keep the team intact. The

where it's headed. This distinction, along with appropriate speech acts, such as declarations, requests, and promises, enables you to steer the conversation in the desired direction. There are seven tips that will help you do this.

When a conversation begins, it will almost always start in the realm of the past. This is normal and, to an extent, good. It is through conversations from the past that we establish relationships and reconnect with people. Indeed, one of the only benefits of past conversations is that second was that he remain neutral and in good standing with both team members throughout the process, and the third was that he wanted me to deal with both parties equitably.

Obviously it is important to me to understand the conditions of satisfaction attached to his request before I acted. If those are not clear, I might take some action in which I would technically grant his request, but he would not get what he *really* wants. Taking this notion to the absurd, I might decide to shoot one of the troublemakers. That would end the divisiveness and meet the original request, but it obviously wouldn't give my client what he wanted.

You might be interested to know that there was a happy ending to this story. I placed separate phone calls to each of the troublesome team members under the auspices of seeking feedback on team performance. Not surprisingly, the issues that concerned the team leader surfaced. This gave me the opportunity to request a lunch meeting with both of them. In this way, I was able to leave the team leader out of the process and facilitate a working agreement. This approach worked because I used *their* concern and commitment to drive my action, rather than the team leader's. It also helped to keep our conversation private. No one had to admit they were wrong or foolish in front of their colleagues.

they create a background of relatedness that makes it easier to work with and communicate with others. What we refer to as "small talk" is a past conversation.

Think about when you meet someone for the first time. What happens? "Oh, you're from Chicago. I lived in Chicago for five years—did you ever meet so-and-so?" Or "So you play golf? Ever played at Bollingbrook?" You talk about the past. Indeed, it's the only thing you can talk about. You just met, so it would be presumptuous of you to immediately talk about the future or make a request. You don't ask someone you just met to baby-sit for you while you're out of town. You don't have a relationship with a new acquaintance, and conversations based on the past are a way of building that relationship.

• *Tip 1: Let the conversation begin and remain in the past for a while before you begin to manage and shift it.*

How long should a conversation stay in the past? That depends on how well connected the participants are. The better you know one another, the more frequently you meet, the less time it needs. You be the judge. Managing conversation is an *art*, not a science.

As you sense that a sufficient background of relatedness has developed, begin to shift the conservation. In most cases, you want the flow of conversation to go from the past to the future and end in the present.

• *Tip 2: Generate both a sufficient number of possibilities and support for one or more of those possibilities before making requests and promises.*

Just as you had to let the conversation stay in the past until relationships were established, you must let the conversation remain in the future long enough to generate a sufficient number of possibilities. It also needs to generate adequate commitment from participants for one or more of the possibilities being created. Here you might use the enrollment process discussed earlier.

• *Tip 3: Continue to generate commitment by facilitating the creation of as many possibilities, options, or approaches as you can.*

As participants get on board, there will be a strong tendency for them to go into action. In this situation, managing conversation means holding the conversation back and keeping it in the future until participants have a sufficient number of choices. Choice is a prerequisite to commitment, and there can be no commitment without choice. One option, regardless of how acceptable it is, will seldom generate true commitment. The emphasis here is on quantity; the quality of possibilities is not particularly important at this point. However, you will want to have at least a couple of good possibilities on the list before you turn to the present.

* *Tip 4: Manage your listening, and as much as possible that of other people, to keep possibilities alive and viable.*

Generating possibilities is often referred to as brainstorming, but most brainstorming is not what it seems. You can conduct a little experiment around brainstorming that may surprise you.

Make a list of ideas and suggestions offered during a brainstorming session. Afterwards, silently point to each suggestion on the list and ask participants to indicate, by raising their hands, which ones they would personally like to explore. What proportion of the ideas do you think a majority of brainstormers agree are good? My experience is usually less than 50 percent. The other suggestions were mentally eliminated in people's heads well before any formal discussion.

There are undoubtedly good possibilities, or the seeds of new possibilities, among the discarded suggestions. And while the rules of brainstorming say that you can't "shoot down" another person's idea, most people do it anyway—in the way they listen. *Reactive listening is the enemy of possibility*, and it must be managed constantly.

You might review the listening management process outlined earlier in Chapter 7. Remember that couching and giving voice to your own judgments and those you suspect in others tends to disempower reactive listening. For instance, you might couch a really radical possibility with, "This idea may seem far out, but I've seen it work before," or "I know you're going to say this approach failed in the past, but I think the time is right now." Remember, the more difference there is between a new possibility and current circumstances, the stronger the negative reactive listening, and the greater the possibility for a breakthrough—which brings us to the next tip.

* *Tip 5: Go for a breakthrough.*

Many of the possibilities that will be offered will involve taking what already exists and making it more, better, or different. If you end up taking action on one of these options, the most you can expect is an incremental improvement. That may be good enough, but you don't have to settle for that.

By focusing the attention and energy of the participants on truly new possibilities, you can help ensure that any action that follows has the potential to make a fundamental change. When you've developed a commitment to one or more possibilities, that brings you to the last step of the conversation.

- *Tip 6: End most conversations in action.*

Through the use of requests, promises, and committed responses you will put activities and processes in motion and turn possibilities into realities. If you have your desired outcomes and conditions for satisfaction in mind, you will be able to quickly and easily negotiate counteroffers. Of course, initiating action and keeping it going are two different things.

- *Tip 7: Follow up on requests and promises and offer coaching to keep action going and overcome breakdowns.*

Few things in life and business go exactly as planned. And if you're going for a breakthrough, they almost never do. You can count on problems and breakdowns. And, with the realization that problems *should be happening,* you are equipped to seek and provide coaching to keep yourself, your team, and your organization moving toward a new and better tomorrow.

Of course, there is more to life than work, and you can apply all the same distinctions, techniques, and processes used in business outside it as well. By changing and managing the way you speak and listen, you can create a new future for yourself and those you care about.

13

CONVERSATION AS A WAY OF LIFE

———

You don't have a work life, a social life, a spiritual life, and a personal life. You live *one* life. To be a successful and fulfilled leader, you must also have a successful and fulfilling life everywhere you go. Mastering conversation enables you to be successful at *everything* you do. The concepts and many of the techniques and processes explored to this point apply as much at home as they do on the job.

In this chapter you will learn about the subtle differences needed when you apply the eight basic conversational principles outside your workplace. In addition, the chapter presents ten keys for developing and maintaining fulfilling long-term relationships.

Listening is important in professional conversations, but even more so in personal ones. Managing your listening becomes paramount away from your job. The first three keys to building and maintaining fulfilling and exciting relationships have to do with they way you listen.

LISTENING *IS* RELATIONSHIP

If there is a place where this elusive thing called "a relationship" lives, it would be in your listening. As a human being, you have many wants and needs. If you make a list, somewhere near the top you will find the need to love and be loved, the need to feel important and valued, and the need to be and feel a part of something more than yourself. These are primal needs and all of them are met through the way you listen to others and the way they listen to you. Let's start with the need to love and be loved.

What is it that makes being in love so fantastic? To a large degree, it is that someone you think is wonderful thinks you are fantastic (so it must be true). Love of others and love of self is all tangled up when we are in love, and seemingly one and the same. Indeed, it is through being loved by someone else that many people come to love themselves. Listening plays a key role in loving and being loved, because the way you see another person and yourself shows up *first* in how you listen, and later in how you speak.

You look at a picture of a loved one and your little voice, the echo of your listening, says, "How wonderful. There's a great-looking, smart, fun, loving person." And when the person you love speaks, you are particularly tuned in to hear expressions of love for you, as well as further evidence that the person is intelligent, exciting, and has all the other qualities that fit through the listening filter you have created around your loved one. It is initially through listening that love manifests, even with someone you may meet for the first time.

While it may be the way a person looks or acts that first draws your attention, it is the conversation in your head, which ensues almost immediately, that begins the relationship. And if you have ever loved from afar, you can begin to appreciate how your little voice can spin a fantastic story. That's what you are doing when you fall in love. You are writing, reading, and listening to a story that *you* created about the other person. So if you want to establish or change a relationship, begin with listening.

When someone really listens to you, it makes you feel important, valued, interesting, likable, intelligent, accepted—all the things you are or are striving to be. When a person listens not only to your words but to your emotion and commitment, you feel close and connected. It would be difficult, if not impossible, not to like or love such a person back.

- *Key 1: If you really want to connect with a person, listen!*

When you meet someone new, while you may make some judgments based on how they look, dress, and act, you are almost starting with a blank sheet, so to speak. That's one of the things that makes new acquaintances and relationships so much fun. Because your listening is almost totally subjective, you are able to create the ideal person. In essence, the process of falling in love is akin to the Pygmalion effect.

If you recall, this process gets its name from the classical Greek story in which Pygmalion, a sculptor, falls in love with the statue of a woman as he works on it. As in George Bernard Shaw's version of *Pygmalion* (later to become the classic musical *My Fair Lady*), Ovid's Pygmalion encounters difficulties during his love affair—once she comes to life and moves out of his studio, his Galatea turns out not to be the perfect mate he thought she would be. In the same fashion, many times the stories we weave as we listen to others create trouble and turmoil for us.

Have you ever met someone you liked, but after a while found yourself thinking or saying, "They're not what they seemed?" You may have been intentionally deceived, but probably not. What happened was that a story you initially wove about this person didn't jibe with who they really were. Your listening created rose-colored glasses through which you perceived this person.

Your listening is not only active in new relationships, but in existing ones as well. In existing relationships, your listening for individuals is well established. However, if you *change* your listening for a person, your relationship will change, because listening drives your behavior.

To change your listening, you can use many of the same processes and techniques discussed earlier to manage your own listening, and shape and change the listening others have for you. Awareness is the key to changing how you listen. Building and improving a personal relationship begins with being aware of the listening you have for a person, particularly the less positive stories.

• *Key 2: Identify the negative listening you have for key people in your life as a way to immediately begin improving your relationships.*

There are many ways you get in touch with your negative listening. You might catch yourself gossiping or talking about a particular person. Note the things you say and think about a person immediately after you've had a disagreement with them. All the worst things we think about people tend to surface when we are angry, upset, or hurt. However, you may only have to heighten your awareness the next time they open their mouth to speak. Remember, listening filters pop up *before* anyone says a word. As your spouse, child, or friend approach and are about to engage you in conversation, what is your little voice saying? Is it saying something like, "What marvelous things have they been up to?" or "Here comes another soap opera." The first is affirmative and the second is reactive listening. Reactive listening limits and ultimately destroys relationships. Awareness is your defense. Once you are aware of your listening, you are able to stop and change it.

• *Key 3: Substitute proactive listening for your reactive listening.*

Reactive listening is *listening to someone*, affirmative listening is *listening for something*. Simply find or invent something positive to listen for when the person in question speaks. It might be caring, compassion, wisdom, coaching for you, anything you'd be glad to find. It may seem strange to make up this listening—until you recall that most of your reactive listening is fabricated anyway. It's difficult for human beings to listen without any filters, so don't fight it. Substitute a listening filter that enhances relationships and generates more possibilities, then watch what happens.

Your listening defines the boundaries and limits of your relationships. You *act* within those boundaries to create your own reality with that person. And, as you have learned, action is created by the way you speak.

SPEAKING AND CREATION

The notion that *everything you create in your life is the result of a conversation* is the fundamental premise of this book. This power to create includes everything, including relationships.

Love, self-worth, and the other things sought in relationships exist in language and are created, maintained—and destroyed—in the way you speak and listen, and through other nonverbal conversation and symbolism.

The notion that love and self-worth exist and show up in language and other forms of conversation first came up in Chapter 9. To build on this awareness and appreciation, think about the many ways you and others signify and express love—letters, greeting cards, poetry, songs, wedding vows, etc. These are different forms of speaking and listening. In addition, you use a host of nonverbal communications such as rings—infinite circles that say "forever"—and photos that say "you belong in my life." Is it any wonder why these seemingly insignificant objects take on so much meaning? They are not only the way we *signify* love, but the way we *create* love.

The process of courting and falling in love is accomplished in conversation. Wooing, romancing, or whatever you want to call it represents the ultimate in managing conversation because it takes place mostly in the present

Listening and the Couch Potato

A woman in one of my workshops seemed puzzled and disturbed as I was discussing how the background listening we have for people in our lives creates reality. She shook her head, which prompted me to ask what was going on.

"You don't know my husband," she said. "It's hard for me to believe that my listening makes him *boring*." The group laughed (but it wasn't funny).

"So your husband's boring?" I asked.

"With a capital B," she said without hesitation.

"If you're willing to do a little experiment, I think you'll better understand the power of listening." I asked this woman to repeat out loud, "My husband is interesting." She had trouble doing this, laughing, shaking her head, and interjecting, "But he's not."

The group was having a good chuckle as I continued to make her say "My husband is interesting" until she could say it with a straight face and the room was quiet. I asked her to keep that notion in mind as she went home tonight, especially when she first encountered her husband. She said she would do this and report what happened to the group the next day.

The next morning, I was just kicking things off when this woman with the "boring" husband raised her hand and be-

and future. Listen to people in love; each speaks about how beautiful, wonderful, and lovable the other *is*—the present—and how great their life together *will be*—the future. You and other people in love speak this way without thinking about it. Imagine what would happen if you began to do it intentionally. Indeed, that's what Valentine's Day is designed to do. If you want to improve your primary relationships, put a little Valentine's Day in every day.

• *Key 4: Create and maintain relationships by continually having and shifting conversations with others into the present and future.*

gan bouncing up and down in her seat. "I've got to tell you what happened last night," she said, visibly excited. I asked her to tell her story.

"Well, there I was all the way home, saying 'My husband's interesting. My husband's interesting.' When I got home and walked into the living room, and there he was . . . planted on the sofa watching TV.

"I have to admit, for a moment, I slipped up and began to see Bob as a boring couch potato; but I hung in there. Like a prayer, I whispered, 'My husband's interesting' as I sat down next to him. I asked him what he was watching.

" 'Star Trek,' he said.

"Normally I would have walked into the kitchen, but I hung in there. 'What's this program about?' I asked.

"Bob looked up, a little surprised. It turns out he'd seen this episode five or six times before. It was about some kind of hole in the space-time continuum. He told me about a bunch of quantum physics stuff . . . and Einstein's theory of relativity. How about that?

"I never knew that kind of stuff was going on in Bob's head. I didn't understand all of what he was saying, but I have to admit, it was interesting . . . he was interesting."

The beautiful thing about mastering the art of conversation is that it enables you to get things done while simultaneously building and maintaining relationships.

In most business and professional conversations, the emphasis is on action and making fundamental change. Maintaining relationships becomes secondary. In most personal conversations, both elements are present, but the emphasis is on (or should be on) establishing and improving the quality of the relationship. Things need to happen in your relationships. You have to get things done, and you can. It's simply a matter of priorities.

• *Key 5: Even when action is imperative in your personal conversations, be cognitive of how your speaking and listening affects your long-term relationship.*

Conversation is the glue that binds people together. The way you listen and speak shapes and influences not only the relationship you have with people close to you, but with all people, places, ideas, and organizations. We are social animals. The need to be and feel a part of something more than oneself is fundamental to human existence. And this need is met primarily through conversation.

BUILDING A BRIDGE TO YOUR ISLAND SELF

You are not your body. This thought undoubtedly occurs to you from time to time. Maybe when you lay injured or ill and you experienced the feeling of being imprisoned. Maybe when someone you liked couldn't see past your physical imperfections. However or whenever it occurs, this notion that your physical body is a capsule in which your true self resides creates a feeling of being separate and alone in the world. This is a scary thought, to say the least. This feeling of separation, and the need and desire to connect with the world around you, drives much of your daily behavior and most all your social behavior.

What is society, after all, but a complex mechanism through which you connect with others. Society is a hierarchy of relationships—couples, families, neighborhoods, cities, states, nationalities, cultures, countries. . . . All these relationships are established and maintained through conversation. Couples exchange vows; countries, like America, are "spoken into existence" through a written declaration. And it is also through conversation—prayer—that people connect with the divine.

These esoteric concepts have a pragmatic application in your life, particularly off the job. The quantity and quality of conversations you have with others will ultimately determine the quality and viability of all your relationships.

Back in Chapter 2, we distinguished a leader as someone whose ultimate objective is sustainability—long-term success. Mastering the art of conversation off the job, and in particular managing your listening, creates healthy, fulfilling long-term relationships.

Using your new distinctions for speaking and listening, you can deepen your connection with the important people in your life. The basic principles are the same: talk about the past only to make an initial connection or resolve incomplete conversations, then shift to the future and end in the present.

BUILDING AND ENHANCING PRIMARY RELATIONSHIPS

Three specific conversation types will do the most to help you build and maintain viable primary relationships: completing the past, coaching, and visioning.

Completing the past, you may recall, breaks down a barrier in relationships. When you feel incomplete, it pulls you away from others. You become *upset,* you're out of balance and unable to proceed smoothly with your life.

You become upset in one of three ways:

- You intended to do something and someone or something stopped you from doing it.
- You expected a particular thing to happen and it didn't.
- You felt something needed to be said and you were unwilling or unable to say it.

Regardless of the cause of the upset, the solution and the process of resolving it begins with a conversation called "completing the past," which was outlined in detail in Chapter 8.

Much of the time, big upsets resolve themselves immediately because they are so traumatic that people cannot withhold their feelings. The upset comes out into the open and people deal with it so they can get on with their lives. Smaller upsets, however, often seem trivial or unimportant. As a result, you may dismiss them without saying anything. These small upsets may seem to go away, but most of them do not. They accumulate under the surface.

Because these suppressed upsets are incomplete transactions, you and others will tend to hold on to most of them. Over time, you carry around what amounts to an enormous gunnysack full of small upsets. These upsets—past conversations—have the effect of keeping your relationship rooted in the past. And, with no future or growth, even the strongest of relationships will fade and eventually die.

• *Key 6: Conduct periodic conversations to clear the air or complete the past.*

Completing the past is a conversation that will likely take place whether or not you make it happen. Have you ever been in a situation where your spouse or significant other became extremely upset at a small comment or minor incident? You probably wondered or said, "What happened?"

In most cases, the minor incident was simply a trigger that allowed old upsets to surface. Not just the last one or two, but *all* of them. The cumulative effect of these seemingly small upsets can make for one big explosion.

The old story about the couple who got a divorce because the husband didn't put the cap on the toothpaste is not as silly as it sounds. It could happen. Of course, the marriage didn't really break up over a capless tube of toothpaste, but over a thousand trivial annoyances—finding the toothpaste uncapped again and again, having to make new sandwiches cut on a diagonal instead of straight across, collecting a drift of lone socks from one end of the house to the other. It might be said that divorce is a form of completing the past, but not a very satisfactory one. Holding conversations specifically to complete the past would be much easier and less traumatic.

Upsets are the primary catalyst for conversations to complete the past, but there are other catalysts as well. Unexpressed appreciation or thanks can make you incomplete, as can acknowledgment you failed either to give or get. Likewise an unexpressed concern or complaint can make you incomplete, or a promise or commitment you wanted to make but didn't—so can lies, gossip, mistakes, hurt feelings. Any time you leave an interaction wishing you'd said or done something, or hadn't said or done something, you will be incomplete.

While it is possible to immediately resolve some upsets and situations internally, most go into your gunnysack waiting for an opportune (or inopportune) time to surface and erupt. But you don't have to wait for a trigger; you can resolve almost any incompleteness with the help of a simple conversation.

Find some quiet time and create a context for completing the past using your own words. You might say, "Something happened awhile back that is bothering me, and I'd like to talk it over with you. And if there are things nagging at you, you can get those off your chest too."

Remember, the objective of this type of conversation is to deliver the previously undelivered communication, not to evoke forgiveness or apology. It's important to make that clear as you start the conversation. Your only expectation is that your companion will *listen*. If an apology or an expression of forgiveness happens naturally, that's great, but don't expect it—that's not part of the deal.

A conversation to complete the past is often two-sided, but that's not a hard and fast rule. In addition, you should have these conversations as soon as you are aware that you are incomplete. Before you leave a meeting or hang up the phone, if you become aware that you are incomplete, say something then and there. Over time, as you become aware of incompleteness in the moment, special conversations will become unnecessary, and you can focus on more proactive and positive conversations like coaching.

• *Key 7: Bring coaching conversations into all your primary relationships.*

The more trust and respect coaches have, the more powerful and effective they are. It would stand to reason then that your spouse or significant other would be a great coach. Of course, they will have to share the same distinction for coaching, otherwise it may become a euphemism for advice or some other type of conversation.

Use the distinction and coaching process outlined in Chapter 6, or create one of your own. *Any conversation that gives the person being coached more confidence in their ability to perform and leaves them poised to act, is a coaching conversation.* As in organizations, coaching conversations are mostly missing in primary relationships, and so is visioning.

• *Key 8: Focus on creating a new future with those you love.*

Creating a vision is not just for organizations; it's for couples, families, and friends as well. If a relationship is to grow, it needs a space to grow into. A vision provides that space.

Life can be so demanding at times that it takes all your energy just to manage day-to-day existence. It's easy to fall into a mode where all your attention and conversations are about what happened and what you and others need to do next. This tendency to live in the past and the present alone is dangerous to relationships. To prosper, relationships need a future—a vision.

A vision as it pertains to a relationship involves planning for the future, but it can be much more. A common complaint among couples who have been together a long time is that their relationship is boring and mundane. This happens because, if you're not careful, your future becomes nothing but a logical extension of the past. Relationships get stuck in the endless cycle, and the result is boredom. Remember the power of possibility and declarations.

How often do you get together with your spouse or significant other to co-create and share a new possibility? Visioning should be a dream, but it should be more than idle daydreaming.

* *Key 9: Go into action on your shared dreams.*

Remember, the conversational pattern: shifting from the past to the future, then to the present. A conversation for possibility should be followed by one for action—make some promises and requests that will turn your dreams into reality.

* *Key 10: Achieve the impossible—live a life of breakthroughs.*

Not everyone is like Forrest Gump, but we can all live his kind of life. As pointed out earlier, the story *Forrest Gump* was about a person who lived a life of breakthroughs. And as weird and fantastic as most of the events in his life were, they seemed believable. That's because they were possible. Without knowing it, Forrest had all the ingredients necessary to create breakthroughs—he had possibility, commitment, and breakdowns. There were plenty of breakdowns in his life. Living a life of breakthroughs isn't all wine and roses, but it's exciting and fulfilling.

It's difficult to achieve breakthroughs by yourself. You need ongoing coaching, support, and new possibilities— things you can get from the important people in your life. You can be more than a couple or a family. You can be a *breakthrough team.*

Of course, for many people this team includes more than just a spouse or significant other. It can and should include your immediate family—particularly the children in or part of your family.

Having Quality Conversations with Children

A newborn child evokes many wonderful feelings. Each new birth sparks the ultimate conversation for possibility.

When you look at a baby you begin thinking and talking about the future. This is not surprising, since the child has little past to speak of. A baby is pure potential. This notion is embodied in the cliché, "That baby could grow up to be president." But what happens to that potential? A few children will grow up to be president of something, and a lot more will end up sleeping in a cardboard box in an alley.

There are many factors that determine how much of a baby's potential is realized, and one of the most significant is the quality of conversation parents and families have with that child.

There are many conversations that help a child, or any person, reach their full potential. Coaching is one that immediately comes to mind. Dialogue and feedback are also essential. In addition, there is no better circumstance in which to apply what you know about breakthroughs.

You might think that lack of experience is a child's greatest limitation, but in reality it is his or her greatest asset. The past does not have the same hold on children as it does on you. You will often hear a boy or girl talk about being an astronaut, explorer, or doctor. When they do, how do you respond? What is often interpreted as daydreaming is actually a declaration of possibility and the first important step in creating a breakthrough. You should take such declarations seriously and engage the child in further conversation for possibility. The child or young person has supplied one of the three ingredients necessary for a breakthrough—possibility. You can help them with the other two, as they build commitment and deal constructively with breakdowns.

Generate and maintain commitment by encouraging the child to share aspirations with other people. The more the better. As you do, be careful to avoid one pitfall. While children's futures may be at stake when they speak about their future plans, your love should never be. Make it clear that your love will be there *no matter what direction the child takes in life.* Remember the power of conversation. Simply end conversations for possibility with statements like "And I'll love you no matter what you do." This simple phrase, repeated over time, will help to maintain the unconditional love every child and person wants and needs. Of course, once people go into action, feedback and dialogue become the conversations needed to facilitate their growth and development.

Feedback is simply periodic talks that enable people to simultaneously get acknowledgment for what they've accomplished and identify areas in which they need to improve. The key to feedback is *balance*. If it is to foster development and growth, feedback must include what's going well and what isn't. One way to ensure balanced feedback is to use a simple three-part process—retain, reduce, increase.

Conduct each feedback conversation by first pointing out things that the child or person is doing well and should *retain*. Next, point out those things they are doing that are not going well—things they should stop doing or *reduce*. Finally, point out things that are going well and should be *increased*. While the order is not critical, it is helpful to sandwich the information that is more difficult to hear between the good stuff.

Balanced feedback is important even when most all your information is positive and affirming. While it is always helpful to give children many verbal pats on the back, difficulties will arise if a child, or any person, gets nothing but positive feedback. Over time, unmixed positive feedback will foster egotism and arrogance, making any future criticism almost impossible to accept and thus limiting growth and development. Related to this notion, dialogue is one of the conversations critical to the development of any child.

You may recall that *dialogue* is a conversation designed to foster learning. Unlike most adults, children naturally engage in dialogue. Children usually initiate dialogues with questions: Why is the sky blue? What makes us hungry? Where did I come from? Too often we tend to give answers to such questions, rather than engaging in the dialogue proposed.

The question, "What makes us hungry?" can lead to new learning, awareness, and appreciation for our bodies. It can lead to new awareness, not only about nutrition, but about the nature of life itself. If you begin to hear a child's questions as invitations to hold a dialogue, you will learn too. More important, you will foster the deep listening and thinking that enables a person to create new knowledge, as opposed to simply gathering and memorizing facts.

Enhancing Relationships with Friends and Family

Everything you've learned to this point will be useful in developing and maintaining close friendships. So, rather than focus on specific types of conversation, it might be more useful to think about exactly what it is that binds you and others together as friends. You might say that common interests are what bring and keep people together. But, if you look deeper, you may find that it is oftentimes *common problems* instead.

The notion that common problems are the glue that binds friendship may be difficult to accept until you begin to reflect on *former* friendships. Not just friendships that have broken off because of differences, but those that simply drifted apart. Maybe you were close friends with a person in your office, and after they took a position in another department or company, your friendship slowly vanished. Maybe you and your spouse were friends with another couple, and when they got divorced you lost contact with one or both of them. Or look what often happens to pairs of couples where one has a child and another does not. Before the child came along, they shared couple problems. After one couple has a child, they now have kid problems they cannot share, and the friendship often suffers as a result.

Of course, not all friendships are based on shared problems. Certainly, such a foundation does not necessarily contribute to either personal growth or sustainability. If you wish to maintain rich long-term friendships, another basis might be useful. How about a future possibility?

Once again, the basic process of shifting conversations from the past to the future and present comes to bear. Problems come from the past. And, if you think about the kinds of conversations you have with some friends, you may find they focus on the past. While there is some benefit to the venting and griping that often ensues when you share problems and frustrations with another person, the majority of these discussions are not helpful. If however, you shift your conversations with friends to focus on future possibilities, you engage yourself and others in creating a new future. This is a more desirable basis upon which to build a friendship.

New possibilities give you the ability to maintain your friendships forever, because one important characteristic of possibilities is that they are infinite. Of course, this is true not only of friendships, but all relationships and life in general. As the saying goes, *anything is possible*—and there is a lot of evidence that this assertion is true.

You have but to look over human history to understand that you, like every other human being, have the power to do what seems impossible. You have the power, in large part, because you can create and maintain conversations that can be shared, not only with friends, family, organizations, and institutions, but with your community and even the entire world. The last chapter will introduce several individuals who managed to do just that.

14

YOU HAVE THE POWER

You already have everything you need to be a successful leader, not just at work or at home, but in your community, country, and world. The great leaders of yesterday and today used the same basic tool available to you—conversation. Whether history's change agents were political leaders, philosophers, religious or spiritual leaders, social activists, artists, scientists, or generals, they used the power of conversation to its full potential.

This final chapter explores the lives of a few great world leaders. In the process, it demonstrates the eight conversational principles outlined in this book at work. Most of the models of leadership spotlighted in this chapter started as ordinary people with no special advantages, and some could have been called disadvantaged. However, they used the power of conversation to make a lasting difference in the world. You can do the same.

APPLYING THE EIGHT
CONVERSATIONAL PRINCIPLES

If you study the world's great leaders, and especially if you study the conversations they created and shared, over and over again you will see eight conversational principles at work. The same principles outlined in this book were intuitively and intentionally used by the world's great leaders to create fundamental and lasting change.

I have chosen eight people who exemplify the leadership role, along with a number of others who offer insight into one aspect of leadership or another. I intentionally selected very different people in very different walks of life to make two important points. First, that leaders come in all shapes, sizes, and types. Second, that conversation includes more than the written and spoken word.

• *Principle 1: Be aware of the power of conversation and pay close attention to how you speak and listen.*

Conversation lives forever. This becomes obvious as you page through history books. Many of the world's great leaders are dead and buried, but what they created lives on. You will also note that historians tend to focus on key conversations great people had—things they wrote, said, painted, performed, or otherwise communicated. That's because conversations create history.

If you look at some of the world's notable political and national leaders from Hammurabi to Thomas Jefferson to Mao Tse-tung, Winston Churchill, and Adolph Hitler, you will see that they all understood the power of conversation and put great care into how they spoke. And while you might hesitate to acknowledge Adolph Hitler as a great leader, there is little doubt that he recognized and used the power of conversation to its maximum. Including Hitler in our list of leaders emphasizes an important point—namely that the power of conversation can be and is used for good or ill. However, the first principle of mastering conversation, being aware of the power of conversation, is well exemplified by Catherine the Great of Russia.

During her reign in the 16th century, Catherine II transformed Russia, taking it from a country struggling for existence to a world power. She understood and used the power of conversation to accomplish this. With an ever watchful eye on the future, Catherine declared, "My people must glorify themselves and their times by looking beyond the old order towards a felicitous, if not quite utopian future."

Like no monarch before her, Catherine the Great used hundreds of royal decrees and edicts to make changes almost overnight. Her correspondent Frau Bielke wrote, "Catherine gave laws with one hand and did needlepoint with the other." Fabled French philosopher Voltaire called her the "great northern lawgiver."

Catherine was successful, in part, because she changed conversations before she changed policy (something for any business leader to think about). A voracious reader herself, she imported thousands of books into Russia and had them translated, printed, and distributed. She housed many of these in the newly established Academy of Science. Western ideas swept through Russia like the Mongol hordes centuries before. She decreed that all boys and girls would be educated beginning at age five, and played a role in determining what subjects they would study and what books they would read. By letting the conversation for change grow among her people before she made changes, she was assured of their acceptance.

To outsiders it appeared that Catherine the Great had enormous power. She would say something and millions of Russians would obey without question. In reality, she used the power of conversation. She introduced Western ideas through books and education and only after people began to accept these ideas did she decree changes.

- *Principle 2: Don't dwell on past-domain conversations; use them to establish a connection and then move on.*

Throughout this book, I've emphasized the point that the term *conversation* covers more than speaking and listening. It can encompass any form of communication, including the visual and performing arts, where the message gets through and has an effect on the recipient.

Although the connection is difficult to see at times, most artists build on the shoulders of artists who came before. However, the great artists used the past as a point of departure rather than as something to imitate. In doing so, these artists broke the endless cycle by creating a totally new possibility, and thus pioneered a new direction in art. Whenever this happens, it initially causes turmoil and problems—particularly for the artist. That is one reason why the lives of many great artists resemble soap operas.

In general, human beings are comfortable living in the past and initially look with disfavor on anyone who tries to change it. This fact is quickly discovered by almost every great artist. Isadora Duncan, who pioneered modern dance, dealt with harsh critics and criticism most of her short life. Likewise, the first plays by Spanish poet and dramatist Federico García Lorca were ridiculed and largely ignored by Madrid society. And today you may even find yourself questioning whether or not giant Campbell's Soup cans, or other works by artist Andy Warhol, are art.

These artists—and countless other writers, painters, dancers, and musicians through time—have had to struggle to make the difficult transition from the past to a new possibility. Ultimately the masters were able to break through and change people's distinction of art forever. Their personal commitment enabled them to prevail and change the conversation. Oftentimes, however, this doesn't happen until after the artist's death. Which brings up a point worth emphasizing, namely that being a leader and shifting the conversation can and will make your life more challenging and stressful and oftentimes more painful. That's the bad news.

The good news is that, if you can remain committed and continue to speak your new possibility, you *will* succeed. Leadership and tenacity go together. You see this principle in the life of every great leader, including that of Hungarian composer Béla Bartók.

Béla Bartók was one of the greatest and most influential composers of the 20th century, but he wasn't an overnight success. Embittered by the reception his early works received, he began to collect Hungarian and other folk music. The familiar rhythms and melodies of beloved folk songs began to influence Bartók's music. The subdued familiarity of old melodies and rhythms intertwined in his compositions began to fascinate local audiences. Bartók used the music of the past to create a connection with people, but then went in many totally new directions.

Over time, Budapest audiences become less hostile to Bartók's music and performances, including his one-act opera *Duke Bluebeard's Castle*, and the ballets *Wooden Prince* and *Miraculous Mandarin*. After that Bartók traveled widely in Europe and the United States, mostly as a pianist.

The stark strength of Bartók's music, particularly the rhythmic drive of his fast movements, derives in large part from the music of ages past. Many of his melodies are based on the old pentatonic (five-tone) scale; however, they took on a new sound when played on the instruments of his day.

The *Piano Sonata* of 1926 initiated Bartók's most fruitful period, and the *Mikrokosmos* and *String Quartet No. 3* and *No. 6* are acclaimed as some of the most important contributions by a 20th-century composer.

It is doubtful we would even know the name Béla Bartók if, early in his career, he had written to please his audiences. Had he done so, he would have been able to make a living. However, Béla Bartók was not content to make a living, he wanted to make a difference. He did that using the eight conversational principles.

• *Principle 3: Be aware of, manage, and change the broad invisible unspoken conversations that determine the way people see and interpret the world.*

You may recall that unspoken conversations are oftentimes unspoken ideas and concepts shared by many people. These conversations tend to describe the way it *is*. Together these unspoken conversations create your paradigm—the "box" you operate in. Because these conversations are taken as "the truth," they are seldom questioned or challenged. However, when they are, the world shakes. No one knows this better than the great scientists like Isaac Newton, Marie Curie, and Albert Einstein, who dramatically changed how we view the universe and our place in it. Indeed, we are still feeling the tremors created by Charles Darwin more than 150 years ago.

Before Darwin changed the conversation, most of the world believed that all animal, plant, and insect species were *immutable*, that is, that they existed today the way they were originally created. While serving as an unpaid naturalist with a scientific team sailing aboard the *Beagle* from 1831 to 1836, he gathered specimens and data that eventually led him to the notion of natural selection and what would ultimately become his theory of evolution. This theory not only put him at odds with much of the scientific community at that time, but most of the Christian doctrine about creation.

Charles Darwin ran headlong into one of the biggest and most far-reaching unspoken conversations in the world. Unchallenged, the questions about where we come from and how we got here rarely surfaced. After the *Origin of Species* was published in 1859, this broad and powerful conversation from the past was given voice by his countless critics and detractors.

Darwin was fully aware that he had taken the challenge of a lifetime. In a letter to Professor T. H. Huxley, he wrote that his theory of natural selection "is not the first, and it will not be the last, of the great questions born of science, which will demand settlement from this generation. The general mind is seething strangely, and to those who watch the signs of the times, it seems plain that this nineteenth century will see revolutions of thought and practice as great as those the sixteenth century witnessed." Charles Darwin might be surprised that his theory is still debated in the 20th century, and will probably be debated in the next. Such is the power of unspoken conversations.

Darwin mastered the art of conversation. His approach was simple. He always referred to his work as a theory, and not as the truth. He patiently enrolled others, usually one at a time. And he always listened patiently to anyone with even the most seemingly insignificant opinion, especially among his critics. Charles Darwin was what might be called a quiet leader. And while leadership is manifested in conversation, that conversation is not necessarily loud and boisterous. Some of the most powerful declarations, requests, and promises are made in hushed tones and whispers.

• *Principle 4: Shift the conversation first from the past to the future and then to the present.*

There is little doubt that history is written more by social activists than by any other type of leader. In most cases, these agents of change grew up without the benefit of rank, privilege, or social status. Indeed, many—like Harriet Tubman, fugitive slave and legendary figure in the Underground Railroad, and Cesar Chavez, son of a migrant worker, who organized and brought national attention to the plight of farm workers—were disadvantaged economically and socially. Others like Mahatma Gandhi and Gloria Steinem were culturally disadvantaged. It is from their personal deprivation that the seeds of their commitment grew. And it was the conversations they started and maintained that made them powerful and effective.

By definition, social activists want to change current conditions and create a dramatically new and different future for themselves and their constituency. It is not surprising, then, that these leaders focus almost all their energy and attention on the future. They shift the conversation from the past to the future, creating in words a totally new possibility. Once this possibility is created, they shift the conversation to the present and put people into action. There was no one better at shifting conversations than Dr. Martin Luther King Jr.

If you study Dr. King's letters and speeches you will find extraordinary examples of managing or shifting conversation. Again and again, King would use past conversation to establish a connection with his listeners and then move on to declare a new future. He would do all this while speaking his personal commitment and thus tapping into and generating commitment in others.

From a jail in Birmingham, Alabama, King wrote, "We were here before the mighty words of the Declaration of Independence were etched across the pages of history. Our forebears labored without wages. They made cotton 'king.' And yet out of a bottomless vitality, they continued to thrive and develop. If the cruelties of slavery could not stop us, the opposition we now face will surely fail. . . . Because the goal of America is freedom, abused and scorned tho' we may be, our destiny is tied up with America's destiny."

The last line echoes a speech made by another great leader, abolitionist and statesman Frederick Douglass. In 1862 Douglass said, "The destiny of the colored American is the destiny of America." The power of conversation transcends time and can exist seemingly forever. Through conversation, the vision of Frederick Douglass and those freedom fighters who came before was kept alive and echoed in the words of Martin Luther King Jr.

During the historic civil rights march on Washington in 1963, King's words were strongly rooted in the future— "I have a dream that my four little children will one day live in a nation where they will be judged not by the color of their skin, but by the content of their character." Like a true leader, over and over again, he spoke of a future that did not yet exist, but was within the grasp of his people. The day before he was assassinated King said, "I want to do God's will. And he's allowed me to go up the mountain. And I've looked over, and I've seen the promised land." King's vision is not yet fully realized, but it is vital and alive in the conversation he began more than 30 years ago.

• *Principle 5: Manage your listening and that of others by couching and by substituting affirmative for reactive listening.*

It seems that war is a recurring historical theme. Political leaders declare wars, and generals fight them. How do you get thousands or even millions of people to engage in battles that will ultimately find many of them dead? It might seem to defy logic, but it points to the power and influence that great generals have had, and to the power of conversation, which is their primary motivational tool. From Alexander the Great to Napoléon Bonaparte and Ulysses S. Grant, you will find the eight conversational principles at work.

Like most leaders and many generals, Douglas MacArthur was a controversial figure. However, not even his most severe critics would deny that his troops were totally committed to him, and that this commitment made it nearly impossible to defeat his forces.

MacArthur had the loyalty and devotion necessary to get his men to march into battle knowing that most of them would die. While you might suspect that this is a rare power, the truth is, you can do it, not just by the way you speak, but by the way you listen and the way you manage the listening of others. Like most great generals, Douglas MacArthur knew that battles were not won by generals, but by the people on the front lines. He made this point in a simple, straightforward way. He commanded from a front-line position.

His men would look up and suddenly there he was. The famous cap, the brown walking stick, the corncob pipe, the ribbonless, sharply pressed shirt, the plain leather jacket, the khaki trousers, and the shining shoes—these constituted MacArthur's trademark. The sight of him suddenly in the jungle gave his troops the lift they needed, and he knew it. On receiving a congressional resolution of gratitude, MacArthur said, "A general is just as good or bad as the troops under his command make him." The way his troops listened to him, not the words he said, gave Douglas MacArthur the power and influence he needed and used to win victory.

• *Principle 6: Distinguish between those things that exist in substance and those that exist in language, and act appropriately.*

Mischief and problems crop up whenever you and others treat the things that exist in language as though they have a physical existence. Great leaders are either consciously or intuitively aware of this, and they act accordingly. The things that exist in substance don't require leadership; they merely need to be managed. *The things that exist in language are the real work of a leader.*

Wars are fought with guns, tanks, and planes—things that exist in substance. However, during times of war, leaders like Franklin D. Roosevelt and Winston Churchill focus as much on creating nationalism, patriotism, and courage—things that exist in language—as on creating the physical implements of war. But nowhere is the power of distinguishing the things that exist in language more apparent than in the work of the great thought leaders and philosophers of the world. From the revered Chinese sage Lao-tzu to René Descartes, John Locke, and Karl Marx, a handful of philosophers have shaped and changed our world forever.

By its very nature, philosophy deals primarily with those elusive things that exist in language—love, existence, consciousness, freedom, happiness, and the like. It is difficult to single out one philosopher who best exemplifies the principles of mastering conversation, but as you compose a list of candidates, Henry David Thoreau would have to be among them. You can see the key conversational principles reflected in his words. For example, with regard to listening: "It takes two to speak the truth, me to speak and the other to listen." Or, with regard to the role and importance of public and private image: "Public opinion is a weak tyrant compared with our own private opinion. What a man thinks of himself, that is which determines, or rather indicates, his fate."

In 1845, Thoreau began a two-year "sabbatical" at Walden Pond, a secluded woodland about two miles from Concord, Massachusetts. Why he went there and what he learned is contained in one of the most revered and widely read books of all time—*Walden.*

Walden is a timeless book and message. It is a shared exploration of life and living, a guide to seeking and finding happiness, fulfillment, and contentment. By living a simple and thoughtful life, Thoreau was able to see that he, and most everyone else, was treating happiness as though it physically existed, as though you could actually gather it up and store it away. The result is "rampant materialism," and a host of problems that plague society.

In his own words, "I went to the woods because I wished to live deliberately, to front only the essential facts of life, and see if I could not learn what it had to teach, and not, when I come to die, discover that I had not lived." You can be *happy, successful,* and *fulfilled,* but only when you realize that those things don't exist as physical substances . . . and act accordingly.

• *Principle 7: Consciously and intentionally manage and shape your own image as someone people listen to attentively.*

Any great leader recognizes the importance of developing, having, and maintaining an image that causes people to listen to what the leader has to say. What matters is what is absorbed, not what is spoken. The more careful the listening, the bigger the conversation. The bigger the conversation, the bigger the difference.

While it would be possible to select any great leader to bring this principle to life, I have chosen one of my personal favorites—Salvador Dali. However you might judge his art, you could not argue with the fact that he was a consummate master when it came to creating and maintaining the proper image. For Dali, of course, the proper image was that of a weirdo nonconformist. Having people think that he was a highly imaginative, strange, neurotic, and off-the-wall person gave Dali the creative freedom he wanted and needed. With such an image, he could do anything—and he did.

If you recall, the basic technique for managing your own public image involves starting a conversation about yourself. After a while people will begin repeating the conversation you started, and they will forget that it began with you. If you dig through Dali's past, you will find a host of memorable image-shaping statements. "There is only one difference between a madman and me. I am not mad." Or from the prologue to one of his many autobiographies, appropriately enough called *Diary of a Genius*: "Democratic societies are unfit for the publication of such thunderous revelations as I am in the habit of making." However, my personal favorite is, "At the age of six I wanted to be a cook. At seven I wanted to be Napoléon. And my ambition has been growing ever since."

Like Dali, I've found it useful to create an image of myself as a bit wacky and off-the-wall. People often remark, "How do you get others to listen to your weird ideas? How do you get away with that?" "Simple," I respond, "They *expect* it from me." I learned from Salvador Dali not only that I could speak my own image into existence but that having a reputation for being a bit odd could be more of a help than a hindrance. After all, breakthroughs and new possibilities sound strange and off-the-wall at first. And that's what I am up to, and I hope you are also—creating breakthroughs.

• *Principle 8: Go for a breakthrough.*

Breakthroughs come in all shapes and sizes, but most of the great leaders in history were responsible for big breakthroughs. That's what makes them great.

• Each leader created a new possibility—one that was dramatically different from the current circumstances.

• Each was able to tap and maintain personal commitment and generate a similar commitment in countless others in order to achieve the objective.

• Each encountered and overcame countless problems and breakdowns along the way.

• And each leader *prevailed*—some for a short period of time, but others prevail today.

Catherine the Great westernized Russia, modernizing agriculture, industry, government, and education. She promoted international trade and expanded the Russian

Empire into the Crimea and fertile lands of the Ukraine. By the time Catherine died in 1796, a modern society was organized and Russia was playing a role in world affairs. Catherine the Great changed the conversation in Russia and about Russia forever. And this from a woman who never learned to speak Russian well, or without an accent.

Douglas MacArthur served in World War I, but he distinguished himself in the Pacific theater during World War II. His sagacious use of combined land, sea, and air forces to outguess and outfight the enemy culminated in the surrender of Japan aboard the *USS Missouri* in Tokyo Bay, at which he officiated. Ironically, while he was a savage warrior, he warned of the dangers and calamity of nuclear warfare. In a broadcast shortly after the atom bomb was dropped on Hiroshima and Nagasaki he said, "We have our last chance. If we do not devise some greater and more equitable system, Armageddon will be at our door."

The Second World War changed America and the world forever, and it was largely through MacArthur's efforts and genius that the United States was able to fight a war on two fronts. Without a doubt, MacArthur was a leader who believed in achieving the impossible.

Charles Darwin said, "What if—" and our perception of ourselves and our place in the universe changed forever. However, it wasn't his contributions so much as his "possibility thinking" that distinguished him as a leader. After all, what is a theory but a possibility that you take a stand for.

Charles Darwin developed countless theories, not only with regard to evolution, but in the fields of geology, botany, zoology, and the then newly emerging field of genetics. Interestingly enough, Darwin never became personally embroiled in the controversy around his theory of natural selection, often referred to as "survival of the fittest." Although he would listen patiently to criticism, he never argued or defended his theories. He seemed to instinctively and intuitively know that such debates were a mostly useless conversation in the past. He had better things to do. Managing and shifting conversation enables you, not only to speak and listen in the future, but live in the future as well.

Salvador Dali changed the way people "listen to" or see the world. That is what great artists and leaders do. Someone once asked me how I know something is art. I reflected that when I am experiencing art, I find myself momentarily suspended in time and thought. My little voice seems to shut up for a while and I become still inside.

When I'm in this often trancelike suspension, I am under the spell of the artist—seeing through the artist's eyes, hearing through her ears, feeling through his senses. Some call this "getting the artist's message," but that phrase makes you look for some deep, hidden meaning. When I look, listen, and feel a work of art, I like to imagine the artist saying, "And the world is this way too."

If the artist is successful, my assumptions about the way the world "is" are suspended. The artist creates a crack in my paradigm or worldview. Once that happens, my whole explanation for "how things are" can disintegrate. I can get "out of my box." I'll just be in another box, but it's a bigger one filled with more possibilities. Not just artists but all leaders make our world a little bigger.

Henry David Thoreau's works call out to people to reject materialism and seek fulfillment in the mind and the spirit. His words continue to speak to us today. Thoreau's life and work has exerted a profound influence on the nation and the world. His essay "Civil Disobedience" inspired Mahatma Gandhi's Indian independence movement and Dr. Martin Luther King Jr.'s crusade for civil rights, and more recently the struggle in South Africa. Thoreau believed each and every person is capable of anything. In his own words from *Walden*, "Man's capacities have never been measured; nor are we to judge of what he can do by any precedents, so little has been tried."

Leaders make a difference by creating possibilities and breakthroughs. They do this through the way they speak and listen. The conversations they start change the world around them, in small and big ways.

When you look for the biggest changes that have taken place in the world, and the people who have caused and sustained fundamental change, you must include spiritual leaders. The great spiritual leaders of the world were consummate masters of the art of conversation. Indeed, many of their conversations live on in the world's sacred texts.

If you explore their lives, you will see the eight conversational principles at work in the lives and writings of Jesus, Mohammed, Moses, Buddha, Chang Tao-ling, Lao-tzu and others. The difference that these leaders have made is beyond explanation and understanding.

It is said in the bible that God created us in his image. Ralph Waldo Emerson defined man as "God in ruins." It may not be surprising then, that like God, you have the power to create. You create through conversation. History is but a small sample of what is possible. You have everything you need to be a great leader—even a world leader. Use the power God gave you. Master the art of conversation.

INDEX